SALES DIGITS

PROVIDENCE MARKETING

In Providence marketing, the main focus is the producer and his products and services as it takes care of the customers' needs and wants.

SALES DIGITS: PROVIDENCE MARKETING

First edition. December 20, 2023.

Written by Eugy Enoch.

Table of Contents

This book is dedicated to every visionary marketer, entrepreneur, and business enthusiast who dares to challenge conventional approaches and seeks transformative strategies. To those who understand the profound impact of authenticity, empathy, and transparency in the realm of marketing, this work is a tribute to your dedication and innovation. May your journey in the dynamic world of commerce be guided by the principles of Providence Marketing, leading to lasting success, meaningful connections, and a legacy of positive change.

PREAMBLE

Dear Readers,

It is with great pleasure that I introduce you to "Providence marketing: A Holistic Approach to Transformative Business." In the ever-evolving landscape of marketing, we will go on a compelling journey to explore a paradigm shift that goes beyond traditional strategies—a journey into the realm of Providence marketing.

In the pages that follow, we will encounter a fresh perspective on the dynamics between marketers and producers, transcending the conventional boundaries that often separate their roles. We will dissect the principles of Providence marketing, unveiling its core philosophies and demonstrating its potential to revolutionize your approach to business.

Providence marketing, as presented in this book, is not just a strategy; it is a mindset, a holistic way of conducting business that places the producer and their offerings at the forefront. The profound insights into this approach empower readers to integrate Providence marketing seamlessly into their strategies, fostering a sense of co-ownership and credibility that extends far beyond traditional marketing techniques.

The book not only outlines the foundational principles of Providence marketing but also provides practical guidance, real-world examples, and actionable steps to help you implement this transformative approach in your own business endeavors. Each chapter is meticulously crafted to offer a comprehensive understanding of the philosophy and a roadmap for successful application.

As you navigate through the chapters, you will discover the power of knowledge fusion, the importance of a producer-centric focus, and the art of effective communication. I invite you to delve into the intricacies of Providence marketing, emphasizing its potential to elevate your business to new heights.

This book is not just a theoretical exploration; it is a practical guide designed to equip you with the tools needed to implement Providence marketing successfully. The examples provided, the questions posed, and the how-to elements woven throughout the narrative are intended to facilitate a profound understanding of the approach and inspire meaningful action.

Eugy Enoch's passion for Providence marketing is evident on every page, and his commitment to sharing this transformative approach shines through. I encourage you to embrace the insights within these pages, challenge your existing perspectives, and embark on a journey towards a more profound connection with your audience and a more meaningful impact on your business.

This book [the fourth title in the series] is an expansion of an earlier book that I wrote and released under the titles "Sales Digits" and "Push Marketing - Sales Digits Guaranteed to Turn your Prospects into Customers" in 2014 and 2015, respectively.

May this book serve as a beacon of inspiration and guidance as you navigate the exciting terrain of Providence marketing.

Warm regards,

Eugy Enoch.

INTRODUCTION

Welcome to the world of Providence marketing—a realm where traditional marketing boundaries dissolve, giving rise to a transformative approach that transcends the conventional roles of marketers and producers. In this introduction, we will go on a trip that will redefine the essence of business strategies, allowing you to investigate a paradigm shift that is out of the usual.

A Paradigm Shift in Marketing

IN THE DYNAMIC LANDSCAPE of business, where strategies continually evolve, the concept of Providence marketing emerges as a beacon of innovation. In contrast to the often-segregated styles of marketers and producers, Providence marketing brings them together in harmony, presenting a unified front to prospects. It is a mindset that recognizes the producer as the focal point, acknowledging the enormous impact their products or services may have on the lives of their customers.

Foundations of Providence marketing

OUR INVESTIGATION BEGINS with a look at the fundamental concepts that govern Providence marketing. We go into the complexities of knowledge fusion, where marketers' and producers' individual styles smoothly mix to generate a message that connects with authenticity. We emphasize the significance of a producer-centric orientation, in which the needs and desires of the consumer become the foundation of marketing efforts. We will investigate further in a later chapter.

Integration for Success

TO IMPLEMENT PROVIDENCE marketing successfully, one must go beyond surface-level understanding. In this section, we unravel the importance of in-depth knowledge about producers, their visions, and the solutions they offer. Effective training and communication become pivotal, ensuring that the marketer not only comprehends but authentically conveys the producer's message. More on this in a later chapter.

Building Credibility and Recruitment

PROVIDENCE MARKETING holds the power to position marketers as co-owners, fostering credibility and opening doors to successful recruitments. This introduction explores how embracing this approach can redefine the dynamics of trust, laying the groundwork for fruitful collaborations. More on this in a later chapter.

Guide to Implementation

AS WE PROGRESS, A COMPREHENSIVE guide unfolds, revealing how to apply Providence marketing in real-world scenarios. We explore the producer's journey, prompting essential questions about their inspiration and the problems they aim to solve. We highlight the impact of solutions, the cost and pain of development, and the transformative power of education and application for prospects. We will also touch this on a later chapter

A Practical and Transformative Journey

THIS BOOK IS NOT A theoretical discourse but a practical guide designed to equip you with the tools needed to implement Providence marketing successfully. Throughout the chapters, you will encounter specific questions, examples, how-to elements, and actionable guides, ensuring that the insights shared become more than concepts—they become catalysts for meaningful change in your business strategies.

As we embark on this journey together, I invite you to immerse yourself in the philosophy of Providence marketing, challenging preconceived notions, and embracing a holistic approach that has the potential to reshape the way you connect with your audience and conduct business.

UNDERSTANDING PROVIDENCE MARKETING

CHAPTER 1
UNDERSTANDING PROVIDENCE MARKETING

Providence marketing isn't just another methodology; it's a profound evolution beyond the conventional boundaries that often compartmentalize the roles of marketers and producers. Picture this: instead of maintaining a mental tug-of-war between the styles of marketers and producers, envision a seamless fusion, a unity that presents a singular, compelling narrative to your prospects. This isn't just a stylistic shift—it's a philosophical departure that places the producer and their offerings at the forefront.

In the landscape of marketing, distinctions define success. This section draws a stark comparison between the established Distinction marketing and the transformative Providence marketing.

The Distinction That Defines Success

PROVIDENCE MARKETING stands out in the delicate dance of marketing approaches by emphasizing the producer. As a practitioner who has seen the ebb and flow of trends, I can tell that success comes in embracing this approach's distinctiveness. The key question is not what the marketing can offer, but what the producer can bring to the forefront with their intimate understanding of customers' requirements and desires.

In the realm of Distinction marketing, the marketer grapples with a mental dichotomy—an attempt to distinguish and separate the styles of marketers and producers. The focus is on maintaining an equal balance between these two entities in the mind of the marketer, presenting a unified front to prospects. However, this equilibrium sometimes can translate into a fragmented message, leaving prospects to decipher the collaboration between the seller/marketer and the producer.

In contrast, Providence marketing introduces a paradigm shift—a seamless fusion of styles where the marketer becomes a conduit for a harmonious narrative. The focus is not on balancing two distinct approaches but on creating a unified story that resonates authentically with the audience. Providence marketing recognizes that the strength lies in blending the marketer's and producer's styles, presenting a cohesive and engaging narrative.

Emphasizing the Shift towards a Producer-Centric Approach

AT THE HEART OF THE above comparison (*'The Distinction That Defines Success'*), is a fundamental shift towards a producer-centric approach within Providence marketing. Distinction marketing often positions marketers and producers as equal players, creating a mental division that may hinder the creation of a unified and compelling narrative. In Providence marketing, the emphasis is on placing the producer at the forefront, recognizing them as the central figure in the marketing narrative.

This shift is not just stylistic but also philosophical—a departure from traditional approaches where marketers often dominate the communication strategy. Providence marketing advocates for unity in diversity, where the distinctive styles of marketers and producers, when seamlessly blended, create a narrative that captivates and engages.

Note: In the vast landscape of marketing, where strategies vie for attention and efficacy, the shift towards a producer-centric approach emerges as a beacon of brilliance. This section reveals the revolutionary nature of Providence marketing by emphasizing the critical movement toward putting the producer first—a shift that not only distinguishes but significantly affects the very fabric of marketing strategies.

Impact on Message Cohesion

THE CONTRAST IN STRATEGIES becomes apparent when examining the impact on message cohesion. In Distinction marketing, maintaining an equal focus on marketers and producers can lead to a disjointed presentation. Prospects may perceive a lack of cohesion in the marketing message, making it challenging to form a unified understanding of the collaboration between the seller/marketer and the producer.

Providence marketing, on the other hand, prioritizes message cohesion by unifying the styles of marketers and producers. The narrative becomes multidimensional, allowing the audience to connect with a story that encapsulates the spirit of both entities. The shift towards a producer-centric approach enhances message clarity and authenticity.

Philosophical Departure

BEYOND THE SURFACE-level differences, there exists a philosophical departure between Distinction marketing and Providence marketing. Distinction marketing often treats marketers and producers as separate entities with equal emphasis. In Providence marketing, the philosophy revolves around recognizing the unique role of the producer and placing them in a central position. It's a departure from a mindset that sees marketers and producers as interchangeable, shifting towards a model that acknowledges and celebrates their distinctive contributions.

Long-Term Implications

CONSIDER THE LONG-TERM implications of these strategies. Distinction marketing may achieve immediate balance, but the risk lies in a lack of cohesion and a potential dilution of the marketing message over time. Providence marketing, by embracing a producer-centric approach, contributes to long-term brand loyalty and advocacy. The recognition of the producer as a central figure creates a strong foundation for building trust, authenticity, and lasting connections with the audience.

In essence, the comparison between Distinction marketing and Providence marketing reveals not only stylistic disparities but fundamental differences in philosophy. While Distinction marketing attempts to balance, Providence marketing seeks to fuse and harmonize, creating a narrative that transcends traditional marketing boundaries.

Real-World Examples

LET ME ILLUSTRATE THIS with a concrete example from the tech industry. Consider a startup that embraced Providence marketing by placing its founder, a visionary in the field, at the forefront of their marketing campaigns. Instead of showcasing features and benefits, the focus was on the founder's journey, the inspiration behind the product, and the transformative impact on users. The result? A surge in customer engagement, loyalty, and a distinctive brand image.

The Mental Tug-of-War

TRADITIONALLY, MARKETERS have navigated a mental tug-of-war, attempting to balance the distinct styles of marketers and producers. The challenge lies in creating a unified narrative that seamlessly incorporates both perspectives. This balancing act often leads to a fragmented presentation to prospects, leaving them to decipher the collaboration between the seller/marketer and the producer. The conventional approach has its merits, but it lacks the cohesion necessary for a truly authentic and compelling message.

Seamless Fusion and Harmonious Narrative

ENTER PROVIDENCE MARKETING—A paradigm shift that dispenses with the mental gymnastics and ushers in a seamless fusion of styles. The emphasis is no longer on keeping a balance between marketing personalities; rather, it is on developing a coherent narrative that resonates authentically with the audience. The transition is from a disconnected, two-dimensional presentation to a multidimensional storytelling that captures the producer's spirit and offerings.

Unity in Diversity

PROVIDENCE MARKETING advocates for unity in diversity, recognizing that the distinctive styles of marketers and producers, when blended seamlessly, create a narrative that captivates and engages. The marketer becomes a conduit, a storyteller who doesn't merely convey features and benefits but narrates a transformative journey—one where the producer takes center stage.

The Producer-Centric Approach Defined

AT THE CORE OF THIS shift is a producer-centric approach that redefines the dynamics between sellers and producers. Unlike traditional methods where the marketer's style may overshadow the producer's contribution, Providence marketing positions the producer as the central figure. It acknowledges that customers are not merely buying a product or service; they are investing in the story behind it. The producer becomes the face, the inspiration, and the driving force of the marketing narrative.

Impact on Prospects' Perceptions

THIS SHIFT HAS PROFOUND implications for how prospects perceive the collaboration between the marketer and the producer. It creates an environment where the prospect envisions a cohesive partnership, a united front working in tandem for their benefit. The prospect no longer navigates a mental dichotomy but is presented with a unified message that resonates with authenticity and credibility.

Building Trust through Authenticity

PROVIDENCE MARKETING'S producer-centric approach is a trust-building mechanism. By spotlighting the producer and their journey, it fosters authenticity and transparency. Customers appreciate the genuine connection, understanding that the marketer isn't just a conduit for sales but a storyteller passionately representing the essence of the producer and their offerings.

Long-Term Impact on Brand Image

BEYOND IMMEDIATE SALES, the shift towards a producer-centric approach leaves an indelible mark on brand image. It cultivates a sense of co-ownership, positioning the marketer not as an intermediary but as a partner in the producer's journey. This approach contributes to long-term brand loyalty and advocacy, as customers connect not just with the product but with the story, the passion, and the authenticity behind it.

In essence, emphasizing the shift towards a producer-centric approach within Providence marketing is an enlightening journey into the heart of authenticity, trust-building, and the profound impact that arises when marketers and producers join forces in a harmonious narrative.

Foundations of Providence Marketing

TO UNDERSTAND PROVIDENCE marketing in its entirety, one must delve into its foundational principles. It begins with Knowledge Fusion—an art where the distinct styles of marketers and producers fuse into a harmonious message. The marketer, armed with in-depth knowledge about the producer(s), their visions, and the very core of the solution, becomes a conduit for authenticity.

The foundation of Providence marketing will be covered in further detail in the following chapter.

In-Depth Analysis

CONSIDER THE SCENARIO where a marketer possesses comprehensive knowledge about a software company's founder—understanding their motivations, the challenges they aimed to overcome, and the vision that fueled their journey. Armed with this deep understanding, the marketer seamlessly integrates this knowledge into their communication strategy, presenting a unified front that resonates with authenticity.

Integration for Unprecedented Success

TO SUCCESSFULLY IMPLEMENT Providence marketing, one must first navigate the terrain of effective training and communication. It is not enough to simply comprehend the information offered by the producer; it is also necessary to internalize it to its very core and honestly communicate the essence to the prospects.

Warnings and Anecdotes

HOWEVER, A WORD OF caution: effective communication isn't about regurgitating information but about embodying the producer's message. I recall a scenario where a marketer, despite having access to exhaustive training material, failed to grasp the emotional core of the producer's journey. The result? A disconnection with the audience, highlighting the critical importance of not just knowing but feeling the narrative.

Building Credibility and Navigating Recruitment

IN THE REALMS OF PROVIDENCE marketing, credibility becomes the cornerstone. As a marketer and salesman who understands the intricacies of building trust, the Providence marketing approach positions you not just as a conduit for sales but as a co-owner—a persona that resonates authenticity, credibility, and influence.

Illustrations from the Internet

CONSIDER THE CASE OF a social media influencer who embraced Providence marketing by aligning with a skincare brand. Instead of a mere endorsement, the influencer became a co-owner of the brand's journey. By sharing the founder's story, personal experiences with the product, and emphasizing the authenticity of the solution, the influencer not only enhanced their credibility but also catalyzed a wave of brand advocates.

The Essence of Providence Marketing

PROVIDENCE MARKETING stands out as a beacon of transforming brilliance in the complicated variety of marketing concepts. This section goes into the heart of Providence marketing, unraveling its essence, while providing a broad picture of the potential impact it can have on the landscape of corporate success.

Core Principles and Philosophy

AT THE HEART OF PROVIDENCE marketing lies a set of core principles that transcend traditional marketing boundaries. These principles form the bedrock upon which the transformative narrative of Providence marketing is built.

Let us consider a list of them:

a. Knowledge Fusion

Providence marketing advocates for Knowledge Fusion—a unique art where the distinct styles of marketers and producers seamlessly fuse into a harmonious message. It's not just about acknowledging the styles; it's about embracing them in a unified story. The marketer, armed with in-depth knowledge about the producer(s), their visions, and the very core of the solution, becomes a conduit for authenticity. Knowledge Fusion is the alchemy that transforms information into a compelling and genuine narrative.

a. Producer-Centric Focus

A fundamental tenet of Providence marketing is its producer-centric focus. Unlike traditional methods where the marketer's style may overshadow the producer's contribution, Providence marketing positions the producer as the central figure. It's an acknowledgment that customers are not merely purchasing a product or service; they are investing in the story behind it. The producer becomes the face, the inspiration, and the driving force of the marketing narrative.

a. Authenticity as a Guiding Light

Authenticity is not just a buzzword in Providence marketing; it's a guiding light. The philosophy revolves around presenting an authentic narrative that resonates with the audience. Customers today crave genuine connections, and Providence marketing positions authenticity as a powerful tool to build trust and credibility. It's about telling a story that goes beyond features and benefits, delving into the essence of the producer and their offerings.

Overview of its Potential Impact on Business Success

PROVIDENCE MARKETING is not just a theoretical construct; it's a dynamic force that has the potential to reshape the trajectory of business success. Let's explore how this innovative approach can leave an indelible mark on the business landscape.

a. Enhanced Customer Engagement

By placing the producer at the forefront and narrating a compelling story, Providence marketing enhances customer engagement. It goes beyond transactional relationships, fostering a connection that resonates with the audience. Customers become not just consumers but advocates, drawn into a narrative that aligns with their values and aspirations.

a. Credibility as a Cornerstone

Credibility becomes the cornerstone of success in Providence marketing. The producer-centric approach positions the marketer not as an intermediary but as a co-owner of the producer's journey. This elevation of status contributes to increased credibility, trust, and a sense of authenticity. Customers are more likely to engage with brands they perceive as trustworthy and genuine.

a. Long-Term Brand Loyalty

Providence marketing is a catalyst for building long-term brand loyalty. By weaving a narrative that transcends individual transactions, it cultivates a sense of co-ownership and allegiance. Customers who connect with the producer's journey are not just patrons; they become advocates, fostering a loyalty that extends beyond the immediate product or service.

a. Elevated Brand Image

Beyond immediate sales, Providence marketing contributes to an elevated brand image. It positions the brand as more than just a provider of goods or services; it becomes a storyteller, an entity that resonates with the human experience. This elevation of the brand image contributes to differentiation in a competitive market, making it more memorable and impactful.

In summary, the essence of Providence marketing lies in its commitment to authenticity, knowledge fusion, and a producer-centric focus. This innovative approach has the potential to redefine not only how businesses market their offerings but also how they establish lasting connections with their audience.

Practical Guide to Implementation

AS WE NAVIGATE THE realm of Providence marketing, a guide unfolds—a guide that is not just theoretical but intensely practical. Real-world examples, actionable steps, and a detailed roadmap are laid out for those who seek not just knowledge but transformation in their marketing strategies.

The Power of Questions

PICTURE THIS: you, as a marketer, armed with a set of questions that prompts the producer to reflect on the core inspiration behind their product or service. These questions, meticulously crafted, serve as beacons that illuminate the transformative narrative, laying the foundation for a compelling marketing strategy.

More on these questions in the Appendices [Appendix B].

Extensive Examination of Problems and Solutions Using Examples

EXPLORE WITH ME THE depth of understanding as we unravel the root causes and challenges that producers sought to address. Providence marketing, at its core, is about offering solutions that transcend mere transactions. Let me share an example about a marketer of a diabetes solution.

Example 1: Transformative Marketing for a Diabetes Management Product

IN THE REALM OF PROVIDENCE marketing, imagine a skilled marketer taking on the challenge of promoting a pharmaceutical company's innovative diabetes management product. The goal is not just to sell a product but to become a trusted ally in the well-being of individuals facing the challenges of diabetes.

How can the marketer achieve this?

a. Understanding the Root Causes:

The marketer conducts extensive research, engaging directly with the diabetes community to comprehend the holistic challenges they encounter. By organizing focus groups, online surveys, and participating in community events, the marketer gains insights into both the physical and emotional aspects of living with diabetes.

a. Crafting Comprehensive Solutions:

Armed with this empathetic understanding, the marketer works closely with the pharmaceutical company to position the product as part of a comprehensive solution. Beyond medication, the offering includes personalized lifestyle guides, educational resources, and mental health support. The aim is to empower individuals, recognizing that successful diabetes management extends beyond mere medication.

a. Engaging the Diabetes Community:

Providence marketing comes alive through community engagement initiatives orchestrated by the marketer. They organize webinars featuring healthcare experts, create online forums for shared experiences, and develop a mobile app for daily support. The marketer ensures that the brand is actively present in the community, participating in conversations and demonstrating a commitment to being more than just a product provider.

a. Narrative-Centric Marketing Campaigns:

Traditional product-centric advertising transforms into narrative-centric storytelling. The marketer collaborates with individuals from the diabetes community to share authentic stories of triumph over challenges. The marketing campaigns emphasize not only the efficacy of the product but also the overall support provided. These narratives resonate with authenticity, building trust and positioning the brand as a reliable companion in the well-being journey.

a. Measuring Impact on Well-Being:

Success metrics extend beyond product sales. The marketer establishes key performance indicators (KPIs) that measure improvements in users' overall well-being. Metrics include lifestyle changes, mental health enhancements, and increased community engagement facilitated by the brand's initiatives.

In this scenario, Providence marketing transforms the marketer from a conventional product promoter to a compassionate ally. The marketer creates a narrative that transcends the transactional by understanding and addressing the tremendous impact of diabetes on individuals' lives, building a sense of collaboration and genuine caring within the diabetic community.

Example 2: Community-Centered Diabetes Care

ANY COMPANY CAN LEVERAGE Providence marketing as a strategic approach to build authentic connections with their audience, establish trust, and differentiate themselves in the market.

Let me share an example from the healthcare industry where a pharmaceutical company, through Providence marketing, can delve into the heart of the health issues faced by the community. By addressing not just symptoms but the profound impact on people's lives, the company can transform from being a mere provider to a trusted ally in well-being.

Imagine a pharmaceutical company specializing in diabetes care that seeks to redefine its role beyond being a traditional provider of medications. This company embarks on a journey to understand the daily challenges and emotional struggles faced by individuals living with diabetes.

How could the marketer company achieve this?

a. Understanding the Root Causes:

The company conducts in-depth research, engaging with the diabetes community to understand not just the physical symptoms but the root causes of the challenges faced. Through surveys, interviews, and community events, they delve into the emotional and lifestyle aspects that influence diabetes management.

a. Developing Comprehensive Solutions:

Armed with this profound understanding, the pharmaceutical company goes beyond developing medications. They create a comprehensive support ecosystem, including educational resources, lifestyle coaching, and mental health support. The focus is not only on addressing symptoms but on empowering individuals to lead fulfilling lives despite their health condition.

a. Community Engagement Initiatives:

Providence marketing comes to life through community engagement initiatives. The company organizes workshops, support groups, and online forums where individuals can share their experiences, challenges, and success stories. The aim is to create a sense of community and mutual support, reinforcing the idea that the company is not just a medication provider but a partner in well-being.

a. Narrative-Centric Marketing Campaigns:

Marketing campaigns shift from traditional product-centric approaches to narrative-centric storytelling. The company shares authentic stories of individuals overcoming diabetes-related challenges, highlighting not only the efficacy of their medications but also the holistic support provided. These narratives become a powerful tool in building trust and positioning the company as a trusted ally in the well-being of the diabetes community.

a. Measurable Impact beyond Medications:

The company measures success not just in terms of medication sales but in the overall well-being of the community. Metrics include improvements in lifestyle, mental health, and community engagement. The impact is not just on physical health but on the quality of life experienced by individuals living with diabetes.

In this example, Providence marketing transforms the pharmaceutical company from a conventional provider to a trusted ally. By understanding and addressing the profound impact of diabetes on individuals' lives, the company establishes a narrative that goes beyond transactions, fostering a sense of partnership and care within the community.

Chapter Conclusion

IN THE JOURNEY OF PROVIDENCE marketing, this chapter serves as a gateway—a gateway to understanding the details, the philosophies, and the actionable steps that propel success.

Our journey began with a comparative analysis of Distinction marketing and Providence marketing. Distinction marketing, with its emphasis on separating the roles of marketer and producer, stands in stark contrast to the transformative paradigm of Providence marketing. In the latter, we witnessed the emergence of a producer-centric approach that redefines the marketer's role, fostering collaboration and co-ownership in the narrative.

As we explored this shift, it became evident that Providence marketing transcends the transactional nature of traditional marketing. It generates a narrative tapestry that resonates with authenticity and establishes a meaningful connection with the audience by connecting the stories of the marketer and the producer.

The Essence of Providence Marketing: Unveiling Core Principles and Potential Impact

MOVING DEEPER INTO the essence of Providence marketing, we uncovered its core principles and philosophy. At the heart of this approach lies a commitment to authenticity, genuine storytelling, and a comprehensive understanding of the producer's journey. The marketer, in embracing these principles, transforms into a storyteller, weaving narratives that go beyond product features to touch the very soul of the audience.

Moreover, the potential impact of Providence marketing on business success cannot be understated. It extends beyond traditional metrics, measuring success in terms of community engagement, brand loyalty, and the genuine improvement in the lives of the audience. As we navigate this terrain, it becomes clear that Providence marketing is not merely a strategy; it's a guiding philosophy that reshapes the very fabric of marketing endeavors.

In Retrospect: The Unfolding Tapestry of Providence Marketing

THIS CHAPTER HAS BEEN a journey of discovery, unearthing the foundational elements of Providence marketing. We've witnessed the metamorphosis from Distinction marketing, observed the emergence of a producer-centric narrative, and grasped the profound impact that authentic storytelling can have on business success.

As we set sail into subsequent chapters, let the lessons learned here serve as a compass. Providence marketing is not just a methodology; it's a narrative journey that invites marketers to become architects of transformative stories. As a marketer and salesman who has witnessed the transformative power of this approach, I invite you to delve deeper into the subsequent chapters, each unlocking a new facet of Providence marketing.

CHAPTER 2
FOUNDATIONS OF PROVIDENCE MARKETING

This chapter serves as the cornerstone—a guide to laying the essential foundations that will support an authentic and transformative narrative. Here, we delve into the profound principles that form the bedrock of Providence marketing, exploring the art of seamlessly integrating marketers' and producers' styles and creating a unified message that resonates with prospects.

Knowledge Fusion

THE COMBINATION OF marketer and producer styles is the key to unleashing the potential of Providence marketing in the wide variety of marketing. Let's take a look at the subtle aspects of Knowledge Fusion, where styles blend, and messages come together.

Knowledge fusion is about bridging styles and unifying messages. Let us examine this concept in details.

Integrating Marketers' and Producers' Styles

IN THE TRADITIONAL realm of marketing, there exists a dichotomy between the styles of marketers and producers. Knowledge Fusion seeks to bridge this gap, encouraging a symbiotic relationship where the distinctiveness of each style merges into a harmonious whole.

Let's look at how to foster this integration, in details:

A. Empathy as a Bridge

Knowledge Fusion begins with empathy. Marketers step into the shoes of producers, understanding their perspectives, challenges, and aspirations. By cultivating a deep sense of empathy, marketers forge a connection that goes beyond the transactional.

The integration of marketers' and producers' styles isn't just a merging of methodologies; it's a profound journey facilitated by the bridge of empathy. This emotional connection becomes the cornerstone, fostering collaboration and mutual understanding between the storytellers and the architects of the narrative.

Empathy's Transformative Role:

Understanding Perspectives: At the heart of empathy lies the ability to understand and appreciate diverse perspectives. Marketers immerse themselves in the world of producers, gaining insights into the challenges, triumphs, and aspirations that shape their narrative. This understanding becomes the compass guiding the collaborative journey.

Shared Emotional Experience: Empathy transcends mere comprehension; it's about sharing an emotional experience. Marketers don't just grasp the technicalities of a product or service; they empathize with the passion, dedication, and emotional investments of the producers. This shared emotional resonance forms the basis for a narrative that speaks to the audience on a profound level.

Cultivating Empathy:

Active Listening: Empathy begins with active listening. Marketers engage in deep, attentive listening sessions with producers, allowing them to express their vision, values, and challenges. By giving producers a platform to articulate their narrative, marketers forge a connection rooted in genuine understanding.

Immersive Experience: Stepping into the shoes of producers involves more than just listening; it's about immersing oneself in their world. Marketers may spend time observing the production process, interacting with key team members, and even experiencing the challenges firsthand. This immersive experience cultivates a level of empathy that goes beyond surface understanding.

Empathy's Impact on Collaboration:

Breaking Down Barriers: Empathy acts as a catalyst for breaking down the barriers that often exist between marketers and producers. When marketers authentically connect with the emotional core of the producer's journey, it creates an environment where ideas flow freely, fostering a collaborative synergy that transcends traditional roles.

Building Trust and Respect: Trust and respect are the pillars of effective collaboration. Through empathy, marketers build trust by demonstrating a genuine commitment to understanding and valuing the producer's perspective. This trust forms the bedrock upon which a unified, authentic message for prospects can be constructed.

The Ripple Effect of Empathy in Narratives:

Authenticity in Storytelling: Empathy infuses authenticity into storytelling. Marketers, having walked in the shoes of producers, convey the narrative with a sincerity that resonates with the audience. The stories told are not just about products or services; they are about the shared human experience that binds producers and consumers.

Connection with the Audience: The empathetic bridge extends beyond the internal collaboration between marketers and producers—it extends to the audience. The authentic narrative, crafted with empathy, creates a connection with the audience as they sense the sincerity and depth embedded in the story. This emotional connection enhances the overall impact of the Providence marketing strategy.

As the bridge of empathy spans the gap between marketers and producers, it sets the stage for a collaborative journey where styles intertwine, ideas converge, and narratives unfold with a richness born of shared understanding. In the realm of Providence marketing, empathy becomes the guiding force that transforms collaboration into a transformative narrative experience.

A. Collaborative Ideation

In the spirit of collaboration, marketers and producers engage in ideation sessions. This collaborative exchange sparks creativity, ensuring that the resulting narrative is a fusion of diverse insights. Ideas flow seamlessly, weaving a narrative that reflects the collective vision.

Let's look at this in more details.

Diverse Perspectives, Unified Vision:

Collaborative Ideation thrives on the synergy of diverse perspectives. Marketers and producers, each bringing their unique insights and experiences to the table, engage in a creative dialogue that transcends traditional roles. The outcome is a unified vision—a narrative that seamlessly integrates the richness of both styles.

Breaking the Silos:

Traditional marketing often operates within silos, with marketers and producers working in isolation. Collaborative Ideation dismantles these silos, fostering an environment where ideas flow freely and barriers between roles dissolve. This collaborative approach ensures that the narrative is not confined by predefined roles but is shaped organically through shared creativity.

Navigating the Ideation Landscape:

Open Dialogue and Communication: At the core of Collaborative Ideation is open dialogue. Marketers initiate meaningful conversations with producers, encouraging them to share their perspectives, aspirations, and even challenges. This open communication creates an atmosphere where ideas are exchanged freely, laying the groundwork for a narrative that authentically represents the producer's journey.

Brainstorming Sessions:

In the spirit of collaboration, brainstorming sessions become a catalyst for innovative thinking. Marketers and producers engage in dynamic sessions where ideas are explored, refined, and expanded upon. This collective brainstorming transcends traditional boundaries, allowing for the emergence of unique concepts that form the basis of the narrative.

Cultivating Creativity and Innovation:

Fostering a Culture of Creativity: Collaborative Ideation is not just a one-time event; it becomes ingrained in the culture of Providence marketing. Marketers nurture an environment that encourages creativity, where every team member—regardless of their role—feels empowered to contribute ideas. This inclusive culture becomes a breeding ground for innovation.

Embracing Risk and Experimentation: Innovation often thrives on risk and experimentation. Collaborative Ideation encourages a mindset where taking calculated risks and experimenting with unconventional ideas is not only accepted but celebrated. This fearless approach results in narratives that break the mold and resonate with audiences in unexpected ways.

The Art of Synergizing Styles:

Intertwining Narratives: Collaborative Ideation is the juncture where marketers and producers blend their stories into a unified whole. The many styles interweave to form a cohesive, honest, and resonant narrative. This tying guarantees that the producer's voice is not dominated, but rather elevated through collaboration.

Balancing Creativity and Strategy: While creativity is at the forefront, Collaborative Ideation also involves strategic thinking. Marketers guide the ideation process with an understanding of market dynamics, audience expectations, and overarching business goals. This balance ensures that the final narrative not only captivates but also aligns with broader strategic objectives.

The Ripple Effect in Unified Messaging:

A Unified Message Emerges: The culmination of Collaborative Ideation is the emergence of a unified message—a message that reflects the collective creativity, insights, and visions of both marketers and producers. This unified message becomes the guiding star, steering the Providence marketing narrative towards authenticity, resonance, and impact.

Empowering Marketers as Storytellers: Through Collaborative Ideation, marketers don't just become facilitators; they become storytellers. The collaborative process empowers marketers to craft narratives that go beyond conventional marketing scripts. It allows them to infuse the story with authenticity and depth, creating a narrative that transcends the ordinary.

As the Collaborative Ideation Symphony unfolds, it becomes a revolutionary force in Providence marketing, where the merger of marketers' and producers' approaches creates storylines that touch emotionally with the audience. This collaboration guarantees that every piece of the narrative is imbued with the richness of multiple viewpoints, resulting in a creative expedition from ideation to unified messaging.

Creating a Unified Message for Prospects

WITH STYLES INTEGRATED, the next stride in Knowledge Fusion is crafting a message that speaks with clarity, resonance, and unity. A unified message emerges as the beacon that guides prospects through a transformative journey.

Clarity in Communication: Providence marketing hinges on clarity. Marketers distill the essence of the producer's vision into a message that is concise, compelling, and easy to understand. The unified message becomes the linchpin, ensuring that prospects grasp the purpose and impact of the narrative.

Resonance with Audience Values: Understanding the values of the target audience is paramount. The unified message resonates with the core values of prospects, creating a connection that transcends the transactional. It's not just about selling a product; it's about aligning with the audience's aspirations and beliefs.

Producer-Centric Focus: Elevating the Producer, Fulfilling Needs

IN THE REALM OF PROVIDENCE marketing, the producer takes center stage. This section navigates through the nuances of a Producer-Centric Focus, where the narrative revolves around the producer, addressing the needs and wants of customers with precision.

Making the Producer the Central Theme

PROVIDENCE MARKETING is a departure from conventional approaches that place the spotlight solely on products or services. Here, the producer becomes the central theme, and their journey becomes the narrative thread that weaves through the entire marketing strategy.

Profound Storytelling: The producer's story is told with authenticity and depth. Marketers become storytellers, unraveling the challenges, inspirations, and transformative moments that define the producer's journey. This storytelling approach creates a narrative tapestry that captivates and resonates.

Humanizing the Producer: Beyond business entities, producers are humanized in the eyes of the audience. Marketers emphasize the human side of the producer, showcasing their passion, dedication, and the personal journey that led to the creation of the product or service.

Addressing Customers' Needs and Wants Effectively

THE PRODUCER-CENTRIC Focus isn't just about storytelling; it's about addressing the real needs and wants of customers in a meaningful way. Providence marketing goes beyond the transactional here, providing solutions that have a deep impact on the audience.

Holistic Solutions: Marketers, armed with an in-depth understanding of the producer's offerings, craft marketing strategies that go beyond product features. The emphasis moves to creating holistic solutions that address customers' multiple requirements and desires, assuring a revolutionary impact.

Empathy-Driven Approach: Through empathy, marketers anticipate and understand the unique needs of customers. This empathy-driven approach forms the basis for tailoring the producer's offerings to meet not just the functional requirements but the emotional and aspirational needs of the audience.

Providence marketing's underpinnings are stripped naked as we explore the complicated pathways of Knowledge Fusion and Producer-Centric Focus. These foundations will serve as a springboard for developing narratives that touch, inspire, and leave an everlasting impact on the hearts and minds of the audience in the chapters that follow.

Chapter Conclusion

IN THE EXPLORATION of Providence marketing's foundational elements, this chapter unfolds essential principles that pave the way for a transformative narrative. We've navigated through Knowledge Fusion and Producer-Centric Focus, uncovering the art of seamlessly integrating marketers' and producers' styles while elevating the producer to the central theme of the story.

Navigating Knowledge Fusion:

Knowledge Fusion acts as the guiding compass for the Providence marketing narrative, showcasing the power of unity. As marketers and producers merge their styles, a harmonious collaboration emerges, resonating with authenticity and depth. The journey commences with empathy, forming a bridge that fosters collaboration and shared understanding.

Collaborative Ideation, the vibrant core of this journey, propels the fusion forward. Diverse ideas collide in a creative dance, shattering silos and nurturing an innovative culture. Collaborative Ideation becomes the crucible where styles intersect via open communication, brainstorming, and an unafraid embracing of innovation.

Producer-Centric Focus:

In the realm of Producer-Centric Focus, we've explored the art of storytelling, where producers' journeys are unveiled with authenticity and depth. The central theme becomes not just the product or service but the human side of the producer—passionate, dedicated, and driven by a profound purpose.

Addressing customers' needs and wants becomes an art form. Holistic solutions that go beyond the transactional, along with an empathy-driven approach, reshape the role of the marketer. It's not just about selling; it's about making a difference in the lives of your clients.

Unity in Diversity:

As we negotiate these fundamental principles, the unity in diversity becomes more apparent. Knowledge Fusion and Producer-Centric Focus merge to form a plot in which marketers become storytellers and producers become important characters. Every piece of the plot is filled with the depth of multiple viewpoints thanks to the collaborative journey.

Empowering Marketers as Storytellers:

Collaborative Ideation empowers marketers not just as facilitators but as storytellers. The unfolding story goes beyond traditional scripts, encapsulating the heart of the producer's journey. It becomes a transforming force that strongly connects with the audience, moving beyond the transactional to forge connections based on common human experiences.

Looking Ahead:

Concluding this chapter, the foundations of Providence marketing are solidly laid. The journey through Knowledge Fusion and Producer-Centric Focus sets the stage for narratives that inspire, resonate, and leave an indelible mark on the hearts and minds of the audience. In the chapters to come, these foundations will serve as the springboard for crafting stories that transcend traditional marketing boundaries, ushering in a new era where authenticity, empathy, and collaboration reign supreme.

Join us as we explore deeper into the world of Providence marketing, with each chapter revealing a new aspect of this transforming method. The adventure has only just begun, and the stories that await will undoubtedly captivate, inspire, and revolutionize the very essence of marketing.

Overview

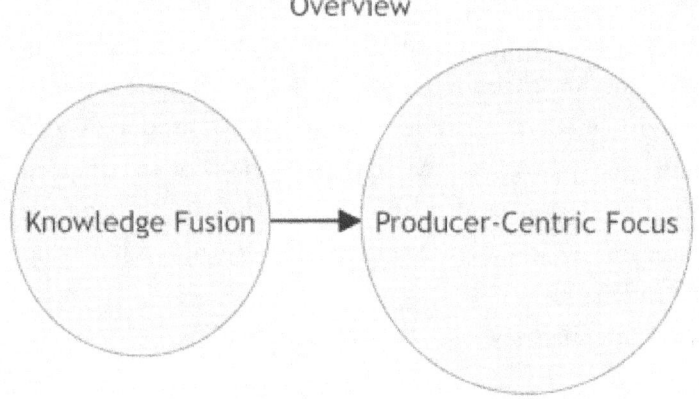

CHAPTER 3
INTEGRATION FOR SUCCESS

The essence of the changing environment of Providence marketing is not just knowing the underlying parts, but managing a seamless integration of these elements for unprecedented achievement.

In the world of Providence marketing, establishing seamless integration necessitates a thorough examination of its fundamental aspects. This chapter goes into the depths of Integration for Success, scrutinizing every element, evaluating data, and drawing on real-world experiences to assist you through this transforming journey as an experienced marketer and salesman.

The Anatomy of Integration

INTEGRATION, IN THE context of Providence marketing, is the strategic fusion of knowledge, empathy, and collaborative ideation into a cohesive narrative. It's the art of weaving the producer-centric focus and marketer's expertise into a storyline that not only captivates but compels action.

Integration hinges on a deep understanding of the producers—the driving forces behind the narrative. We explore the critical importance of comprehending the visions and missions of producers. Real-world examples abound, demonstrating how aligning marketing strategies with producer values amplifies authenticity.

Let's dissect this anatomy for a deeper understanding.

1. Data-Driven Insights

The integration journey commences with a meticulous analysis of data. Dive into market trends, consumer behavior, and competitor landscapes. Uncover insights that illuminate the path forward. For instance, consider a case where a tech company, through integrated data analysis, identified emerging needs in their target market, leading to the development of a groundbreaking solution.

Let's embark on a comprehensive exploration, drawing from years of expertise, data analytics, and proven results to unravel this critical aspect.

Picture this: You, as a seasoned marketer, armed with a wealth of experience, delve into the ocean of data, extracting pearls of insights that illuminate the path forward. Data-Driven Insights become more than just numbers; they are strategic imperatives that inform every facet of the integration journey.

Understanding Consumer Behavior:

The first layer of analysis delves into understanding consumer behavior at a granular level. Real-world examples showcase instances where companies, armed with insights into the preferences and buying patterns of their audience, tailored their integration strategies to align seamlessly with consumer expectations.

Market Trends and Competitor Landscapes:

As a seasoned professional, you recognize the significance of dissecting market trends and competitor landscapes. Anecdotes abound, highlighting cautionary tales of companies that overlooked emerging trends and success stories of those who strategically positioned themselves by leveraging data to gain a competitive advantage.

Predictive Analytics:

The integration journey isn't just about reacting to current trends; it's about anticipating future shifts. Data analytics becomes a crystal ball, offering glimpses into what lies ahead. Warnings echo through cautionary tales where companies failed to heed predictive analytics and suffered the consequences, contrasting with tales of those who successfully navigated the winds of change.

Customer Segmentation and Personalization:

In the age of personalization, Data-Driven Insights empower marketers to tailor narratives to specific customer segments. Dive into examples where companies effectively segmented their audience, delivering personalized experiences that resonated deeply. Warnings emerge of the pitfalls of generic messaging that fails to connect on a personal level.

Conversion Optimization:

Data isn't merely about quantity; it's about quality. Conversion optimization becomes the north star, guiding marketers toward strategies that transform leads into loyal customers. Illustrations showcase the impact of data-driven optimization on conversion rates, contrasting with cautionary tales of missed opportunities due to oversight.

Risk Mitigation:

Integration isn't without risks, and a seasoned professional recognizes the importance of risk mitigation through data analysis. Real-world anecdotes expose scenarios where companies, blindsided by unforeseen risks, faced setbacks, alongside stories of those who navigated potential pitfalls with foresight and strategic planning.

Operational Efficiency:

Data-Driven Insights extend beyond the external landscape to optimize internal operations. Illustrative examples delve into how companies streamlined processes, enhanced efficiency, and reduced costs through data-informed decision-making. Warnings resonate from instances where operational inefficiencies eroded the benefits of integration.

A Personal Touch:

Amidst the logical analyses, remember that data isn't just about numbers; it's about people. Infuse a personal touch by sharing stories of how companies, armed with insights into their audience's preferences and pain points, crafted narratives that resonated emotionally. Emphasize the emotional impact of understanding the human side behind the data.

Measuring Impact:

Data-Driven Insights culminate in impact measurement. Metrics become the barometers of success, and as a seasoned marketer, share examples of companies that meticulously tracked the impact of integrated narratives on brand perception, customer engagement, and revenue. While measuring impact, I will caution against the pitfall of overlooking comprehensive metrics.

As we conclude this deep dive into Data-Driven Insights, remember that in the world of Providence marketing, data isn't a mere tool; it's the compass that guides the integration journey. It's the difference between informed decisions and blind leaps.

1. Aligning Visions

Integration thrives when visions align seamlessly. The symbiotic relationship between visionaries amplifies the authenticity of the narrative. Let's explore this section some more.

The Strategic Essence:

Imagine this scenario: You, as a seasoned professional, recognize the strategic essence of aligning visions. It's not merely a superficial collaboration but a deep-rooted commitment to shared values and aspirations that permeate every layer of the integration journey.

Understanding Producers' Visions and Missions:

At the heart of aligning visions lies a profound understanding of producers—the architects of the narrative. Real-world examples illustrate instances where companies, armed with insights into the visions and missions of their producers, forged alliances that resonated authentically with their audience.

Building Trust through Alignment:

In Providence marketing, trust is non-negotiable. Aligning visions becomes the bedrock upon which trust is built. Dive into illustrations of companies that, through aligned visions, fostered a sense of trust and loyalty among their audience. Cautionary tales echo the repercussions of fractured trust due to misalignment.

Fostering Authenticity in Narratives:

Authenticity is the lifeblood of successful integration, and aligning visions breathes life into narratives. Real-world examples showcase companies that authentically integrated producers' visions into their storytelling, resulting in narratives that felt genuine and resonant. Warnings echo of narratives that rang hollow due to a lack of genuine alignment.

Incorporating Producer Perspectives:

As a seasoned marketer, emphasize the importance of incorporating producer perspectives into the integration narrative. Caution against the pitfall of overshadowing producers' voices in the pursuit of a unified narrative.

Examples of businesses have set themselves apart by valuing and highlighting the distinctive viewpoints of creators.

These narratives act as lighthouses, shedding light on the importance of producer-centric storytelling and authenticity in differentiating oneself in a competitive market.

a. A Local Artisanal Bakery:

Unique Perspective: The bakery, run by passionate artisans, decided to showcase the personal stories and creative journeys of each baker.

Narrative Approach: Instead of generic marketing, the bakery featured video profiles of the bakers, sharing their inspirations, challenges, and the love they infuse into their creations.

Impact: This producer-centric approach not only differentiated the bakery in a saturated market but also fostered a sense of connection between consumers and the creators behind each delightful pastry.

a. Craft Brewery's Brewmaster Series:

Unique Perspective: A craft brewery recognized the expertise and passion of its brewmaster, a seasoned professional with a wealth of brewing knowledge.

Narrative Approach: The brewery launched a "Brewmaster Series" that highlighted the journey of the brewmaster, his philosophies on crafting unique beers, and the stories behind each brew.

Impact: By celebrating the brewmaster's perspective, the brewery elevated its brand, attracting beer enthusiasts who appreciated the authenticity and craftsmanship behind each brew.

a. Tech Startup Amplifying Developer Stories:

Unique Perspective: A tech startup acknowledged the crucial role of its software developers in creating innovative solutions.

Narrative Approach: The company created a blog series and podcast featuring in-depth interviews with developers, exploring their backgrounds, challenges, and the inspiration behind their coding choices.

Impact: By putting the spotlight on the people behind the code, the startup humanized its brand, attracting developers and businesses alike who resonated with the authentic stories shared.

a. Fashion Brand Showcasing Artisan Craftsmanship:

Unique Perspective: A fashion brand collaborated with local artisans to produce handcrafted clothing items, recognizing the expertise and cultural significance of traditional craftsmanship.

Narrative Approach: The brand's marketing campaigns featured not only the final products but also the artisans at work, their cultural influences, and the heritage embedded in each piece.

Impact: This producer-centric approach positioned the brand as a champion of craftsmanship, appealing to consumers seeking unique, culturally rich fashion alternatives.

a. Family-Owned Winery's Vineyard Chronicles:

Unique Perspective: A family-owned winery understood the deep connection between its wines and the vineyards, recognizing the expertise passed down through generations.

Narrative Approach: The winery created a series of videos and social media content showcasing the family's journey, the meticulous vineyard care, and the traditions that shaped their winemaking.

Impact: By sharing the intimate stories of the family and vineyard, the winery cultivated a loyal customer base that appreciated the authenticity and legacy embedded in each bottle.

These stories underscore the transformative impact of embracing producers' perspectives in crafting narratives that resonate. By highlighting the unique stories behind products and services, these companies not only stood out but also created meaningful connections with consumers who value authenticity and the human touch in their choices.

Examples of Successful Partnerships Based on Shared Values and Visions

a. Ben & Jerry's and Fair Trade Certification:

Shared Values: Both Ben & Jerry's and Fair Trade share a commitment to social responsibility, sustainability, and fair treatment of farmers.

Partnership: Ben & Jerry's entered into partnerships with Fair Trade organizations to ensure that the ingredients in their ice cream, such as cocoa and vanilla, are sourced ethically.

Impact: This alignment resulted in a product line that not only resonates with socially conscious consumers but also contributes to the well-being of farmers and communities worldwide.

a. Patagonia and 1% for the Planet:

Shared Values: Patagonia and 1% for the Planet share a commitment to environmental conservation and sustainability.

Partnership: Patagonia, a renowned outdoor clothing company, is a member of 1% for the Planet, pledging at least 1% of their sales to environmental causes.

Impact: This partnership not only aligns with Patagonia's values but also fosters a positive brand image, attracting environmentally conscious consumers who appreciate the company's dedication to making a difference.

a. Tom's of Maine and TerraCycle:

Shared Values: Tom's of Maine and TerraCycle both prioritize eco-friendly practices and waste reduction.

Partnership: Tom's of Maine partnered with TerraCycle to create a recycling program for oral care product packaging. Consumers can send in their used products for recycling, aligning with both companies' commitment to sustainability.

Impact: This partnership reinforces the shared values of environmental responsibility and provides consumers with a tangible way to contribute to waste reduction.

a. Starbucks and Conservation International:

Shared Values: Starbucks and Conservation International share a commitment to ethical sourcing, together, both organizations contribute to the sustainability of the coffee industry, ensuring that coffee production is environmentally friendly and benefits local communities.

a. Unilever's Sustainable Living Brands:

Shared Values: Unilever's Sustainable Living Brands, such as Dove and Ben & Jerry's, share a commitment to sustainability and social responsibility.

Partnership: Unilever's approach involves transforming its brands to align with sustainable living principles, aiming to enhance social and environmental impact.

Impact: By integrating shared values across its diverse portfolio, Unilever not only meets consumer expectations but also drives positive change by promoting responsible business practices.

These examples demonstrate that successful partnerships grounded in shared values and visions can create a win-win scenario. They showcase how companies, by aligning their core values, can amplify their impact on society, gain consumer trust, and contribute to a more sustainable and ethical business landscape.

In conclusion, as we conclude this deep exploration of Aligning Visions, remember that in the world of Providence marketing, alignment is not a static achievement; it's a continuous commitment to shared values and aspirations. Join me in the next chapter as we continue our expedition, delving into the tactical intricacies of Implementation Excellence—a phase where aligned visions transform into tangible, impactful narratives.

Navigating Integration Challenges

THE INTEGRATION JOURNEY is not without its challenges. Drawing from experiences across industries, we navigate potential pitfalls such as misalignment of visions, internal silos, and divergent styles. Solutions emerge, offering a roadmap for overcoming challenges and steering the integration process toward success.

As businesses embark on the journey of Providence marketing, they may encounter a range of challenges that require strategic navigation. Successful integration hinges on addressing these challenges with resilience, adaptability, and a commitment to aligning marketers and producers seamlessly. Here's a deeper exploration of key challenges and effective strategies for navigating them:

1. Misalignment of Visions and Values:

CHALLENGE: Misalignment between the visions and values of marketers and producers can hinder effective collaboration.

Strategy: Facilitate open dialogues and workshops to establish a shared understanding of core values and long-term visions. Encourage mutual respect for each other's perspectives, fostering a collaborative environment.

2. Communication Gaps:

CHALLENGE: Ineffective communication can lead to misunderstandings and hinder the conveyance of the producer's narrative to marketers and, subsequently, to the audience.

Strategy: Implement clear communication channels, including regular meetings, feedback sessions, and collaborative platforms. Foster a culture of transparency, ensuring that both marketers and producers are on the same page throughout the integration process.

3. Resistance to Change:

CHALLENGE: Resistance from internal teams or stakeholders who are accustomed to traditional marketing approaches can impede the adoption of the producer-centric model.

Strategy: Provide comprehensive training programs to educate teams about the benefits of Providence marketing. Showcase success stories and tangible outcomes to build confidence and overcome resistance. Emphasize the positive impact on brand credibility and customer loyalty.

4. Lack of Producer Involvement:

CHALLENGE: Limited engagement from producers in the marketing process can result in an incomplete or diluted narrative.

Strategy: Actively involve producers in marketing strategies, ensuring their authentic voice is heard. Facilitate workshops for producers to share insights, anecdotes, and unique perspectives that can enhance the storytelling process.

5. Balancing Data and Narrative:

CHALLENGE: Striking the right balance between data-driven insights and compelling narratives can be challenging.

Strategy: Develop a framework that integrates data analytics with storytelling techniques. Use data to identify customer preferences and behaviors, allowing marketers to tailor narratives that resonate effectively. Combine quantitative insights with qualitative storytelling for a holistic approach.

6. Maintaining Consistency Across Channels:

CHALLENGE: Ensuring consistency in the producer-centric narrative across various marketing channels can be complex.

Strategy: Implement a robust content strategy that aligns with the core narrative. Provide guidelines and resources to marketing teams to maintain a cohesive brand story across platforms. Regularly review and adapt strategies based on performance metrics and audience feedback.

7. Adapting to Evolving Trends:

CHALLENGE: Rapid changes in market trends and consumer behavior may require constant adaptation of Providence marketing strategies.

Strategy: Foster an agile mindset within the organization. Stay informed about industry trends and emerging technologies. Regularly reassess and adjust marketing approaches to remain relevant and responsive to evolving consumer preferences.

8. Measuring Impact and ROI:

CHALLENGE: Quantifying the impact of Providence marketing and demonstrating return on investment can be challenging.

Strategy: Establish key performance indicators (KPIs) aligned with the overarching goals of Providence marketing. Leverage analytics tools to track metrics such as customer engagement, brand loyalty, and conversion rates. Conduct regular assessments to refine strategies based on performance data.

By proactively addressing these integration challenges, businesses can navigate the complexities of Providence marketing, ensuring a harmonious blend of marketer and producer perspectives to create impactful narratives and foster long-term success.

Providence Marketing in Action

BRING THE INTEGRATION process to life by sharing real-world examples of Providence marketing in action. Illustrate how companies effectively integrated knowledge, empathy, and collaborative ideation to craft narratives that left a lasting impact.

Providence marketing comes to life when the theoretical framework is translated into real-world practices. Let's delve into scenarios where businesses have embraced this approach, showcasing how it unfolds in action, resonates with audiences, and transforms the way brands engage with their markets.

1. Tech Company Humanizing Innovation:

APPROACH: A technology company decided to shift from merely promoting features to humanizing its innovations. Instead of focusing solely on product specifications, the company integrated the stories of the engineers, developers, and designers who contributed to the creation of cutting-edge solutions.

Outcome: This producer-centric approach not only made the technology more relatable but also established an emotional connection with users. Customers began to see the faces and stories behind the products, fostering trust and brand loyalty.

2. Fitness Brand's Journey with Athletes:

APPROACH: A fitness brand reimagined its marketing by centering its narrative around the journey of the athletes who use their products. Through documentaries, social media features, and interviews, the brand shared the challenges, triumphs, and dedication of athletes who relied on their fitness gear.

Outcome: This approach elevated the brand beyond a mere purveyor of workout equipment. It became a companion in the athletes' quests for excellence. Customers resonated with the authenticity of the stories, resulting in increased brand advocacy and a stronger community.

3. Automotive Manufacturer's Craftsmanship Chronicles:

APPROACH: An automotive manufacturer decided to emphasize the craftsmanship behind its vehicles. Instead of generic commercials, the company launched a video series highlighting the meticulous work of engineers, designers, and assembly line workers.

Outcome: Consumers gained insight into the passion and dedication invested in every car. This transparency not only differentiated the brand but also attracted customers who appreciated the artistry and precision involved in the manufacturing process.

4. Eco-Friendly Fashion Label's Sustainable Stories:

APPROACH: A fashion label committed to sustainability integrated Providence marketing by sharing stories of the artisans and communities involved in crafting eco-friendly clothing. The brand showcased the environmental impact of their practices and the positive changes they were making.

Outcome: Consumers aligned with the brand's values, making purchasing decisions based on a deeper understanding of the ethical and sustainable practices. The brand's commitment to transparency and positive impact became a key driver of customer loyalty.

5. Food and Beverage Company's Culinary Chronicles:

APPROACH: A food and beverage company transformed its marketing strategy by focusing on the culinary journeys of chefs and farmers. Through a multimedia campaign, the company shared the stories of those responsible for creating the ingredients and preparing the dishes.

Outcome: This approach elevated the perceived quality of the products by showcasing the passion and expertise behind the scenes. Customers were not just buying food; they were partaking in a narrative of culinary excellence.

6. Financial Institution's Community Impact Stories:

APPROACH: A bank shifted its marketing from conventional financial promotions to narratives highlighting its impact on local communities. Through documentaries and testimonials, the bank showcased the positive changes resulting from its investments in community development.

Outcome: Customers began to see the bank as a partner in community well-being. This producer-centric strategy not only enhanced the bank's reputation but also attracted socially conscious customers who valued the institution's commitment to making a positive impact.

In each of these instances, Providence marketing unfolded as a dynamic and adaptive strategy, allowing businesses to connect with their audiences on a profound level. By integrating the narratives of producers, whether engineers, athletes, artisans, or communities, these brands transcended traditional marketing, fostering authentic connections and redefining the way they engage with their markets.

The Role of Emotional Resonance

Integration transcends the rational; it delves into the emotional terrain. Narrate instances where emotional resonance became a driving force.

In the realm of marketing, some brands have mastered the art of integrated storytelling, creating narratives that resonate deeply with their audiences. These stories go beyond transactions, forging emotional connections that translate into enduring loyalty and fervent advocacy. Let's explore notable examples where brands have successfully woven narratives that stand as powerful testaments to the impact of integrated storytelling:

Nike: "Just Do It" Campaign

Storytelling Focus: Nike's "Just Do It" campaign is an iconic example of integrated storytelling. By featuring real athletes and individuals overcoming personal challenges, Nike communicated a powerful message of determination, resilience, and the pursuit of excellence.

Impact: The campaign resonated not just as a promotion of athletic wear but as a call to action for anyone facing obstacles. Nike transformed into a brand associated with empowerment and the triumph of the human spirit, fostering deep emotional connections with its global audience.

Coca-Cola: "Share a Coke"

Storytelling Focus: Coca-Cola's "Share a Coke" campaign personalized its products by featuring popular names on the labels. This simple yet effective approach aimed to create a sense of personal connection and shared moments among consumers.

Impact: By encouraging people to share a Coke with friends, family, or even strangers with their names on the bottles, Coca-Cola tapped into the universal desire for connection. The campaign resulted in increased sales and a lasting emotional tie with consumers.

Dove: Real Beauty Campaign

Storytelling Focus: Dove's Real Beauty Campaign challenged traditional beauty standards by featuring real women with diverse body types and appearances. The campaign aimed to redefine beauty and promote self-confidence.

Impact: Dove's commitment to authentic representation struck a chord with audiences globally. The campaign not only boosted sales but also positioned Dove as a brand advocating for inclusivity and self-acceptance, fostering a loyal community of consumers.

Apple: "Shot on iPhone"

Storytelling Focus: Apple's "Shot on iPhone" campaign turned customers into storytellers by showcasing user-generated content captured with iPhones. The campaign emphasized the power of technology in capturing and sharing life's moments.

Impact: By featuring real stories and experiences of iPhone users, Apple created a narrative around the product's capability to document and celebrate the richness of everyday life. This approach strengthened the emotional connection between consumers and the brand.

Starbucks: "Meet Me at Starbucks"

Storytelling Focus: Starbucks' "Meet Me at Starbucks" campaign provided glimpses into the lives of people meeting at Starbucks locations around the world. The campaign aimed to capture the coffeehouse as a hub for human connection and shared moments.

Impact: By emphasizing the communal aspect of the coffee experience, Starbucks fostered a sense of belonging and social connection. The campaign contributed to the perception of Starbucks as a space where meaningful conversations and relationships unfold.

Google: "Year in Search"

Storytelling Focus: Google's annual "Year in Search" videos compile the most searched topics and events of the year. The videos encapsulate the collective experiences, challenges, and triumphs of humanity.

Impact: Google's storytelling approach transcends product promotion, reflecting the shared human experiences and emotions captured through online searches. The yearly videos evoke empathy and connection, reinforcing Google's role in facilitating global connectivity.

These brands showcase the power of integrated storytelling in building emotional connections that extend beyond transactions. By authentically tapping into the human experience, they have cultivated loyal communities of advocates who not only consume their products but also identify with the brand's values and narratives.

Measuring Success

INTEGRATION IS MEANINGLESS without measurable success. Let us begin by looking at some indicators for evaluating Providence marketing effectiveness.

Metrics and Key Performance Indicators (KPIs) for Evaluating Providence Marketing Effectiveness

PROVIDENCE MARKETING strategies must be evaluated using a more sophisticated methodology than just standard KPIs. This innovative marketing paradigm emphasizes storytelling, producer-centric narratives, and emotional connections. Here are key metrics and KPIs to consider when evaluating the success of a Providence marketing strategy:

Audience Engagement Metrics:

Comments and Shares: Monitor the volume and sentiment of audience comments on Providence marketing content. Additionally, track the number of shares, as it indicates the content's resonance and the audience's willingness to amplify the narrative.

Brand Sentiment Analysis:

Social Listening: Leverage social listening tools to gauge overall brand sentiment. Analyze online conversations and mentions related to the Providence marketing campaign to understand how audiences perceive the brand and its narrative.

Content Consumption Metrics:

Time Spent on Content: Measure the average time users spend engaging with Providence marketing content. Longer durations suggest deeper interest and involvement with the narrative.

Conversion Metrics:

Conversion Rates: Track conversion rates associated with Providence marketing campaigns. This includes sign-ups, purchases, or any desired actions. A rise in conversions indicates the effectiveness of the narrative in driving consumer behavior.

Customer Journey Analytics:

Attribution Models: Employ attribution models to understand how Providence marketing contributes to different touchpoints along the customer journey. This helps identify the narrative's impact at various stages of the decision-making process.

Brand Loyalty and Advocacy:

Repeat Engagement: Measure the frequency of repeat engagements with Providence marketing content. Consistent return visits indicate sustained interest and potential brand loyalty.

Brand Advocacy: Track the number of brand mentions by users who become advocates and share the narrative independently. This showcases the campaign's ability to inspire brand ambassadors.

Story Impact Metrics:

Narrative Resonance: Assess the resonance of the narrative by analyzing the emotional impact it has on the audience. Surveys, interviews, and sentiment analysis can provide insights into how well the story connects with individuals.

Social Impact Metrics:

Social Change Indicators: For campaigns with a social impact focus, measure indicators related to positive change or awareness in the community. This could include shifts in public perception, policy changes, or community engagement.

Producer Involvement Metrics:

Producer Participation: Gauge the level of involvement and participation of producers in the marketing process. Assess whether producers actively contribute to the narrative and engage with the audience.

Customer Experience Metrics:

Customer Satisfaction (CSAT): Use CSAT surveys to measure the satisfaction of customers who have engaged with Providence marketing content. High CSAT scores indicate a positive customer experience tied to the narrative.

Long-Term Impact Metrics:

Brand Equity: Monitor shifts in brand equity over time. Assess how Providence marketing contributes to long-term brand perceptions, trust, and overall brand strength.

Story Resonance Surveys:

Surveys and Focus Groups: Conduct surveys and focus groups to gather qualitative feedback on the Providence marketing narrative. Understand how well the story is remembered, its impact, and its influence on brand perception.

By integrating these metrics into your evaluation framework, you can gain a comprehensive understanding of how Providence marketing is resonating with your audience, driving engagement, and contributing to long-term brand success. These indicators go beyond traditional ROI metrics, offering a more nuanced perspective on the narrative's impact on consumer behavior and brand perception.

Next, let's look at examples where companies harnessed data analytics to measure the impact of integrated narratives on brand perception, customer engagement, and ultimately, revenue.

Examples where companies harnessed data analytics to measure the impact of integrated narratives on brand perception, customer engagement, and ultimately, revenue.

IN THE ERA OF INTEGRATED narratives, several forward-thinking companies have embraced data analytics to measure the impact of their stories on brand perception, customer engagement, and revenue. Here are examples of companies harnessing data analytics to evaluate the effectiveness of their integrated narratives:

Airbnb: Personalized Recommendations through Data:

Approach: Airbnb employs data analytics to understand user preferences and behaviors. By analyzing the data generated from user searches, bookings, and reviews, Airbnb tailors its narrative to provide personalized recommendations and experiences.

Impact: The personalized approach enhances user engagement by aligning the narrative with individual preferences. Through analytics, Airbnb has been able to increase customer satisfaction, loyalty, and revenue by delivering relevant and compelling stories.

Netflix: Viewer Data Shaping Original Content:

Approach: Netflix relies heavily on viewer data to shape its original content. The streaming giant analyzes user viewing habits, ratings, and interactions to create narratives that resonate with specific audience segments.

Impact: By leveraging data analytics, Netflix produces content that aligns with viewer preferences, leading to increased viewership and subscriber retention. The platform's success in creating binge-worthy series is a testament to the power of data-driven storytelling.

Amazon: Personalized Shopping Journeys:

Approach: Amazon employs data analytics to understand individual shopping behaviors. The e-commerce giant tailors its narrative by recommending products based on users' browsing history, purchase patterns, and preferences.

Impact: By delivering a personalized shopping experience, Amazon enhances customer engagement and satisfaction. The data-driven approach contributes to increased conversion rates and revenue as customers find narratives that align with their needs.

Spotify: Curated Playlists and Storytelling:

Approach: Spotify utilizes data analytics to curate personalized playlists for users. By analyzing listening habits, genres, and mood preferences, Spotify crafts narratives that resonate with diverse audiences.

Impact: The personalized playlists enhance the overall user experience, keeping listeners engaged and immersed in stories told through music. This data-driven approach contributes to increased user retention and premium subscriptions.

Google: Tailoring Search Narratives with User Intent:

Approach: Google employs sophisticated algorithms to understand user intent when conducting searches. By analyzing search patterns and behavior, Google tailors search results to provide narratives that directly align with what users are seeking.

Impact: The data-driven approach enhances the relevance of search results, improving user satisfaction. Google's success in delivering personalized and contextually relevant narratives has solidified its position as the leading search engine.

Starbucks: Personalized Loyalty Program Narratives:

Approach: Starbucks utilizes data analytics through its loyalty program to understand individual customer preferences. By analyzing purchase history and preferences, Starbucks crafts personalized narratives and offers for its loyalty program members.

Impact: The personalized approach strengthens customer loyalty, leading to increased engagement and repeat business. Starbucks' ability to connect with customers on a personal level through data-driven narratives contributes to sustained revenue growth.

Disney+: Data-Informed Content Creation:

Approach: Disney+ leverages data analytics to inform content creation decisions. By analyzing audience demographics, preferences, and viewing habits, Disney+ tailors its content lineup to cater to diverse segments.

Impact: The platform's success in attracting a broad audience and generating buzz around specific content reflects the effectiveness of data-driven narrative decisions. Disney+ uses analytics to align its storytelling with what resonates most with its viewers.

These examples illustrate how companies across various industries leverage data analytics to measure the impact of their integrated narratives. By understanding user behaviors, preferences, and interactions, these companies craft narratives that resonate with their audiences, ultimately driving brand perception, customer engagement, and revenue growth.

Strategic Alliances

AS A MARKETER WITH a wealth of connections, emphasize the importance of strategic alliances in the integration journey.

1. Anecdotes of Collaborative Success: Stories of Enriched Narratives and Expanded Market Reach.

NIKE AND APPLE: FUELING Workouts with Technology:

Collaboration Story: Nike and Apple joined forces to create the Nike+ app, seamlessly integrating technology with athletic experiences. The collaboration allowed users to track their runs and workouts while enjoying personalized playlists through Apple Music.

Impact: The partnership enriched the narrative of fitness by combining sportswear with cutting-edge technology. The collaboration expanded market reach by attracting both Nike and Apple enthusiasts, fostering a community of fitness enthusiasts who valued the intersection of performance and innovation.

Red Bull and GoPro: Elevating Extreme Sports Narratives:

Collaboration Story: Red Bull and GoPro collaborated to capture breathtaking footage of extreme sports events sponsored by Red Bull. GoPro's cameras were integrated into the equipment of athletes, providing immersive perspectives of adrenaline-pumping moments.

Impact: The collaboration enriched the narrative of extreme sports by offering unparalleled visual experiences. It expanded market reach by engaging audiences interested in both energy drinks and action-packed content. The partnership created a unique blend of lifestyle and adventure, resonating with thrill-seekers worldwide.

Starbucks and Spotify: Personalized Coffeehouse Playlists:

Collaboration Story: Starbucks partnered with Spotify to integrate music streaming into the Starbucks app. Customers could influence in-store playlists, and baristas curated playlists based on customer preferences gathered through the Starbucks Rewards program.

Impact: The collaboration enriched the narrative of the Starbucks coffeehouse experience by incorporating personalized music. It expanded market reach by attracting music lovers seeking a unique and customizable coffeehouse ambiance. The partnership created a synergistic blend of coffee culture and music enjoyment.

Tesla and SpaceX: The Elon Musk Ecosystem:

Collaboration Story: Elon Musk, the visionary behind Tesla and SpaceX, created a narrative that transcends individual companies. The collaboration between Tesla's electric vehicles and SpaceX's aerospace endeavors positioned Musk's ventures as interconnected components of a broader vision for the future.

Impact: The collaboration enriched the narrative of innovation and sustainability. It expanded market reach by attracting tech enthusiasts, environmentalists, and those intrigued by space exploration. The Elon Musk ecosystem created a unique brand identity that resonates with individuals interested in the convergence of technology and space exploration.

IKEA and LEGO: Playful Home Furnishing:

Collaboration Story: IKEA and LEGO collaborated to create a range of storage solutions that double as play areas for LEGO enthusiasts. The collaboration brought playful design elements into home furnishings, encouraging creativity and imagination.

Impact: The collaboration enriched the narrative of home furnishing by adding a playful and interactive dimension. It expanded market reach by appealing to families, LEGO enthusiasts, and individuals seeking functional yet creative living spaces. The partnership created a blend of practicality and entertainment within the home environment.

Apple and Hermès: Luxury Meets Technology:

Collaboration Story: Apple collaborated with luxury brand Hermès to create a line of exclusive Apple Watch bands. The collaboration combined Apple's cutting-edge technology with Hermès' craftsmanship and design aesthetics.

Impact: The collaboration enriched the narrative of wearables by introducing a luxury element. It expanded market reach by attracting consumers interested in both high-end fashion and advanced technology. The partnership created a premium niche within the smartwatch market.

These anecdotes illustrate how collaborations between diverse brands can enrich narratives and reach new audiences. By merging different strengths and brand identities, these partnerships created synergies that resonated with consumers, leading to expanded market reach and heightened brand appeal.

2. Insights on the art of forging alliances that complement and amplify each partner's strengths.

STRATEGIC ALLIANCES are a powerful tool for businesses to enhance their capabilities, expand their reach, and create synergies that amplify strengths. Here are key insights into the art of forging alliances that complement and amplify each partner's strengths:

Identify Complementary Strengths:

Insight: Successful alliances start with a clear understanding of each partner's strengths and weaknesses. Identify areas where partners complement each other, bringing unique expertise, resources, or market access to the table.

Leverage Shared Values and Vision:

Insight: Aligning on shared values and a common vision is crucial for a successful alliance. When partners have a shared understanding of their long-term goals and values, it strengthens the foundation of the partnership and fosters collaboration.

Focus on Mutual Benefit:

Insight: A successful alliance is built on mutual benefit. Each partner should gain value from the collaboration, whether it's in terms of increased market share, access to new technologies, cost savings, or enhanced capabilities. A win-win approach is essential.

Create Clear Objectives and Agreements:

Insight: Define clear and measurable objectives for the alliance. Establish agreements and expectations upfront to avoid misunderstandings later on. Clearly outline roles, responsibilities, and the desired outcomes to ensure alignment.

Build Trust and Open Communication:

Insight: Trust is the cornerstone of any successful alliance. Foster open and transparent communication channels between partners. Establishing trust allows for more effective problem-solving, collaboration, and a resilient partnership.

Invest in Relationship Building:

Insight: Building strong relationships at both the personal and organizational levels is essential. Regular communication, joint activities, and face-to-face interactions help strengthen the bond between partners. A solid relationship provides a foundation for navigating challenges.

Adaptability and Flexibility:

Insight: Business environments are dynamic, and adaptability is key. Successful alliances require partners to be flexible and adaptable to changing circumstances. This includes adjusting strategies, realigning goals, and evolving together to meet market demands.

Leverage Technology and Data:

Insight: Embrace technology and data-driven insights to optimize alliance strategies. Utilize analytics to understand market trends, consumer behavior, and performance metrics. This data-driven approach enhances decision-making and ensures the alliance remains relevant.

Mitigate Risks Through Contingency Planning:

Insight: Identify potential risks and challenges early in the alliance formation process. Develop contingency plans to mitigate these risks. Being proactive in risk management enhances the alliance's resilience and ability to navigate uncertainties.

Encourage Innovation and Collaboration:

Insight: Foster an environment that encourages innovation and collaboration. An alliance that embraces new ideas and shared creativity can lead to breakthrough solutions, product offerings, or business models that benefit both partners.

Measure and Evaluate Performance:

Insight: Establish key performance indicators (KPIs) to measure the success of the alliance. Regularly evaluate performance against these metrics, seeking continuous improvement. Assessing outcomes allows for strategic adjustments and ensures the alliance remains aligned with its objectives.

Plan for the Long-Term:

Insight: Strategic alliances are most effective when viewed as long-term partnerships. While short-term gains are important, cultivating a relationship with a long-term perspective allows partners to weather challenges, capitalize on opportunities, and grow together over time.

By incorporating these insights, businesses can navigate the complexities of forming strategic alliances successfully. The art lies in the thoughtful orchestration of partnerships that not only complement each other's strengths but also amplify the collective impact, resulting in sustained mutual growth and success.

Warnings and Preemptive Measures

WHILE STRATEGIC ALLIANCES hold great potential for mutual growth, it's crucial to be aware of potential pitfalls. Here are warnings and preemptive measures to navigate common challenges in forming and maintaining alliances:

1. Misaligned Objectives:

WARNING: Misalignment in objectives can derail an alliance. If partners have different goals or expectations, it can lead to conflicts and hinder progress.

Preemptive Measures: Clearly define and communicate objectives from the outset. Regularly revisit and align goals to accommodate changes in the business landscape.

2. Cultural Misfit:

WARNING: Cultural differences between partnering organizations can lead to misunderstandings, communication breakdowns, and a lack of cohesion.

Preemptive Measures: Prioritize cultural fit when selecting alliance partners. Foster cross-cultural understanding through joint training programs and cultural exchange initiatives.

3. Communication Breakdowns:

WARNING: Ineffective communication can result in misunderstandings, delays, and missed opportunities. Poor communication may also lead to trust issues between partners.

Preemptive Measures: Establish robust communication channels, encourage transparency, and conduct regular check-ins. Clearly define reporting structures and ensure that key information flows freely.

4. Unequal Contribution:

WARNING: If one partner perceives that the other is not contributing equally, resentment can arise, damaging the alliance.

Preemptive Measures: Outline expectations regarding contributions, responsibilities, and resource allocation. Regularly assess and adjust contributions to maintain a fair balance.

5. Lack of Flexibility:

WARNING: Rigidity in adapting to changing circumstances can hinder the alliance's ability to navigate evolving market dynamics.

Preemptive Measures: Foster a culture of adaptability. Embrace flexibility in strategies, operations, and decision-making processes. Regularly reassess the alliance's relevance in the current business landscape.

6. Intellectual Property Concerns:

WARNING: The sharing of intellectual property may pose risks if not adequately protected. Concerns about data security and ownership may arise.

Preemptive Measures: Clearly define intellectual property rights and confidentiality agreements. Implement robust cybersecurity measures to safeguard sensitive information.

7. Dependency Risks:

WARNING: Overreliance on one partner can pose risks if that partner faces financial instability, changes in leadership, or operational challenges.

Preemptive Measures: Diversify dependencies where possible. Develop contingency plans to mitigate risks associated with overdependence on a single partner.

8. Lack of Exit Strategy:

WARNING: Without a well-defined exit strategy, ending an alliance can be messy and may lead to legal disputes or damage to both organizations.

Preemptive Measures: Include a clear exit strategy in the initial alliance agreement. Define conditions under which the alliance can be dissolved and outline the process for transitioning out.

9. Failure to Anticipate Change:

WARNING: Ignoring industry shifts, economic changes, or technological advancements can render the alliance obsolete.

Preemptive Measures: Establish mechanisms for monitoring industry trends and conducting regular strategic reviews. Anticipate change and be ready to adapt the alliance's goals and strategies accordingly.

10. Inadequate Risk Management:

WARNING: Failure to identify and manage risks effectively can lead to unforeseen challenges that jeopardize the alliance's success.

Preemptive Measures: Conduct thorough risk assessments at the alliance's inception and regularly review risk management strategies. Develop contingency plans for potential risks.

By heeding these warnings and implementing preemptive measures, organizations can proactively address challenges, strengthen their alliances, and ensure sustained success in collaborative ventures. Vigilance, open communication, and strategic planning are essential elements in navigating the intricate landscape of strategic partnerships.

Chapter Conclusion

AS WE CONCLUDE THIS exploration of Integration for Success, remember that Providence marketing is not a static strategy; it's a dynamic journey that evolves with the ever-shifting sands of consumer preferences and market dynamics. Armed with knowledge, empathy, and collaborative ideation, companies can not only weather the storms of change but emerge stronger and more resonant than ever.

Join me in the next chapter as we delve into the tactical intricacies of Implementation Excellence—a phase where theories transform into tangible, impactful narratives that leave an indelible mark on the minds of the audience.

PROVIDENCE MARKETING IMPLEMENTATION

CHAPTER 4
BUILDING CREDIBILITY AND RECRUITMENT

Building credibility in the complex world of Providence marketing is more than just establishing trust; it's about constructing a narrative that connects, inspires, and drives people to join the adventure. As a seasoned marketer and salesperson, I've seen the transformative impact of credibility in not only enticing prospects but also creating a legion of committed advocates. Let's go into the depths of this vital chapter and discover the art and science of establishing credibility and recruiting.

Building credibility starts with constructing an engaging story that goes beyond the transactional and into the human experience. Consider the story of a software business created by a group of people who have all overcome industry hurdles. They didn't just sell items by honestly articulating their journey; they sold a story of resilience, ingenuity, and a shared vision for the future.

Real-World Example: Apple's "Think Different" campaign not only showcased their products but also narrated a story of rebels, misfits, and visionaries, establishing credibility by associating the brand with those who dared to challenge the status quo.

Positioning oneself as a co-owner is not only a strategic move in the world of Providence marketing; it is the cornerstone of establishing unrivaled reputation. As we progress through this chapter, we'll look at how to use Providence marketing to create a sense of shared ownership, as well as the tremendous impact it has on recruiting and the subtle dynamics of sub-recruitment attempts.

The Anatomy of Credibility

Foundations of Trust:

CREDIBILITY RESTS ON a foundation of authenticity, consistency, and a demonstrated commitment to values. Analyzing successful brands reveals a consistent alignment between their proclaimed values and their actions. For instance, a sustainable fashion brand gains credibility by not only championing eco-friendly practices but consistently implementing them throughout their supply chain.

Warning: Inconsistency in actions and values erodes credibility faster than any marketing effort can build it. To avoid this pitfall, organizations must conduct regular internal audits to ensure alignment.

Unveiling Providence Marketing's Credibility Arsenal

The Co-Owner's Mantle:

POSITIONING ONESELF as a co-owner involves donning a mantle of shared responsibility and vision. Providence marketing, with its emphasis on authentic narratives and values, becomes the catalyst for this transformation. By aligning personal goals with the overarching mission, marketers elevate themselves from mere sellers to co-owners of a purpose-driven journey.

Strategic Leveraging: A case study in the fashion industry revealed that marketers who embraced the co-owner mindset not only conveyed authenticity in their marketing efforts but also showcased a deeper understanding of the brand's ethos, enhancing their credibility in the eyes of prospects.

The Ripple Effect on Recruitment

Recruitment Redefined:

THE IMPACT OF POSITIONING as a co-owner extends beyond personal credibility—it ripples through the fabric of recruitment efforts. Prospects, sensing a shared commitment, are not just enticed by the product or opportunity; they are drawn to the prospect of becoming co-owners themselves. The recruitment narrative shifts from a transactional pitch to an invitation to join a transformative journey.

Real-world Influence: A direct sales company experienced a surge in recruitment when its representatives, positioned as co-owners, shared stories of personal growth within the company. Prospects, inspired by these narratives, saw recruitment as an invitation to embark on a similar path of empowerment.

Recruitment through Shared Ownership

THE CO-OWNERSHIP ILLUSION:

Recruitment in Providence marketing is more than acquiring team members; it's about fostering a sense of shared ownership. When prospects perceive themselves as co-owners of a mission, recruitment becomes a natural extension of credibility. This approach, often seen in successful MLM companies, builds on the idea that every recruit isn't just a salesperson but an ambassador with a stake in the overarching narrative.

Illustration: Imagine a skincare brand where recruits aren't just selling products but are seen as co-owners of a movement promoting self-love and confidence. Their role extends beyond transactions; they become advocates for a shared philosophy.

Authenticity in Recruitment

Spotlight on the Real:

RECRUITMENT EFFORTS must showcase the real stories of individuals whose lives have been genuinely impacted. Authenticity in testimonials and success stories resonates far more powerfully than scripted narratives. By featuring unfiltered accounts of individuals who found purpose and success through the Providence marketing approach, credibility skyrockets.

Anecdote: A health and wellness company saw exponential growth when they shifted from polished testimonials to raw, unscripted video stories of customers attesting to real transformations.

Warning: The Pitfalls of Overpromising

The Tightrope of Promises:

WHILE BUILDING CREDIBILITY, the temptation to overpromise lurks on the horizon. This perilous tightrope can lead to disappointment and skepticism if not navigated carefully. Honesty about both the benefits and limitations of the products or opportunities is paramount.

Real-world Caution: A financial education company faced backlash when promises of instant wealth overshadowed the realistic timeline for returns. The fallout damaged both credibility and recruitment efforts.

The Recruitment Playbook

Strategies for Success:

RECRUITMENT IN PROVIDENCE marketing requires a well-crafted playbook. This involves targeted communication, personalized onboarding processes, and continuous support for new recruits. The playbook should be a living document, adapting to industry trends and feedback from the field.

Example: A direct sales company enhanced recruitment by implementing a mentorship program, pairing new recruits with seasoned members who guided them through their initial challenges and successes.

Analyzing the Data: Recruitment Metrics

Beyond Numbers:

IN THE DATA-DRIVEN landscape of recruitment, it's crucial to move beyond quantitative metrics and delve into qualitative insights. Monitoring not just the number of recruits but also their engagement, satisfaction, and longevity provides a comprehensive view of recruitment success.

Key Metric: A skincare brand tracked the success of recruits not just by sales but by their ability to convey the brand story authentically. This qualitative metric proved instrumental in predicting long-term recruitment success.

Emotional Resonance in Recruitment

Beyond Transactions:

RECRUITMENT IS AN EMOTIONAL journey. Successful recruitment doesn't merely involve selling an opportunity; it's about creating an emotional connection with the mission. When recruits feel emotionally invested, they become genuine advocates, extending the Providence marketing narrative organically.

In Practice: An educational platform saw increased recruitment by emphasizing not just the career opportunities but the chance to be part of a community dedicated to lifelong learning and growth.

Sub-Recruitment Unveiled

The Art of Sub-Recruitment:

SUB-RECRUITMENT, THE intricate process of inspiring recruits to become recruiters themselves, finds its foundation in the co-owner paradigm. As co-owners, marketers become natural advocates, sharing not just the product but the narrative of empowerment and shared success. Sub-recruitment flourishes when the co-owner ethos permeates the entire marketing ecosystem.

Strategic Cascading: A health and wellness company achieved remarkable sub-recruitment success by fostering a culture where co-ownership was celebrated. Marketers, already positioned as co-owners, effortlessly inspired their recruits to embrace the same ethos, creating a domino effect of shared ownership.

The Co-Owner's Toolkit

Strategies for Success:

POSITIONING AS A CO-owner requires a toolkit that blends authenticity, passion, and strategic communication. Leveraging the Providence marketing approach involves crafting narratives that transcend products, focusing on shared values and aspirations. Co-owners strategically use testimonials, success stories, and personal anecdotes to weave a tapestry of authenticity.

Illustrative Approach: An educational platform empowered its co-owners with a toolkit that included not just product knowledge but also storytelling techniques. This approach enhanced their ability to position themselves as co-owners in every interaction.

Warning: Pitfalls in Co-Ownership Positioning

Navigating Challenges:

WHILE POSITIONING AS a co-owner is a powerful strategy, pitfalls exist. Overemphasis on personal success stories without genuine connection to the broader mission can lead to skepticism. It's essential to strike a balance between personal narratives and the collective journey.

Real-world Caution: A wellness brand faced challenges when marketers overly highlighted personal achievements without emphasizing the brand's overarching mission. This led to a perception of individualism rather than shared ownership.

Chapter Conclusion

IN CONCLUSION, AS WE navigate the terrain of co-ownership positioning in Providence marketing, remember that it's not just a role; it's a mindset. The co-owner paradigm transforms marketers into torchbearers of a shared narrative, influencing not only personal credibility but reshaping the entire recruitment landscape.

Do remember that every interaction is an opportunity to craft a narrative that transcends transactions. It's about building a community of advocates who see themselves not just as recruits but as co-owners of a transformative journey. In the chapters to come, we'll look at the strategic details that raise Providence marketing to the level of an art form, where credibility and recruitment are inseparably linked.

The representation outlines the main sections within this chapter. Each box represents a specific subtopic or section, and the arrows indicate the logical flow from one topic to the next. The "Positioning as a Co-Owner" is introduced, and it branches into two subsections discussing leveraging Providence Marketing to build credibility and its impact on recruitment efforts.

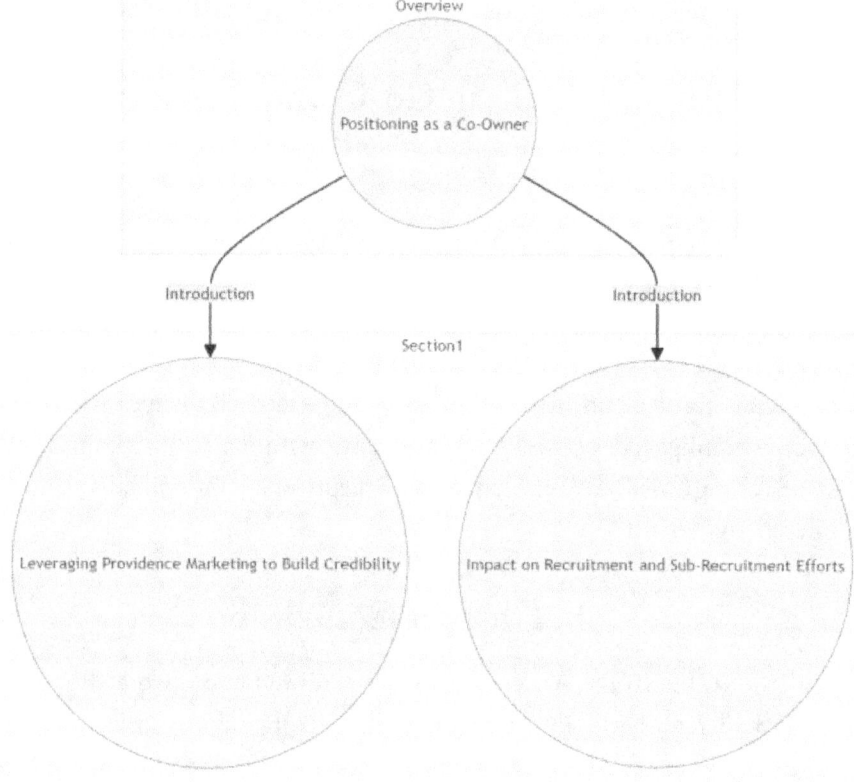

CHAPTER 5
GUIDE TO PROVIDENCE MARKETING IMPLEMENTATION

Embarking on the journey of Providence marketing implementation is akin to navigating a vast ocean of opportunities, challenges, and transformative potential. As a seasoned marketer and salesman, I invite you to join me in this comprehensive guide where we'll unravel the intricacies of Providence marketing, exploring strategies, insights, and real-world examples to pave the way for successful implementation.

The Strategic Foundations

Understanding the Producer's Essence:

BEFORE DIVING INTO implementation, it's imperative to grasp the essence of the producer's vision and mission. Providence marketing thrives on an intimate understanding of the producer(s), their motivations, and the driving force behind the product or service. This foundational insight serves as the compass guiding every subsequent step.

Understanding the Problem

DEVELOPING QUESTIONS for Uncovering Root Causes:
Begin the implementation journey by delving into the producer's journey. Uncover the pivotal moments, challenges, and breakthroughs that gave birth to the solution.

The essence of Providence marketing lies in understanding the problem deeply. Develop questions that go beyond surface-level issues, prompting the producer to reflect on the root causes and challenges. Uncover the intricacies that led to the birth of the solution.

Craft questions that prompt the producer to reflect on the core inspiration behind their product or service. Crafting these questions is essential for unraveling the narrative of Providence marketing. These questions are designed to delve into the deeper motivations and driving forces that led to the creation of their offerings. Here are some thought-provoking prompts:

Inception:

- What was the pivotal moment or inspiration that sparked the idea for your product or service?
- Can you trace back to the initial seed of thought that led to the creation of your offering?

Personal Connection:

- How does your personal journey or experiences contribute to the inspiration behind your product or service?
- Were there specific life events that influenced your decision to develop this particular solution?

Mission and Values:

- What core values and principles drive your company's mission, and how do they align with the creation of your product or service?
- Can you share insights into the ethical or moral considerations that shape your approach?

Solving a Problem:

- What specific problem or challenge in your life or the lives of others motivated you to create this solution?
- In what ways does your product or service address a gap or fulfill a need in the market?

Vision for Impact:

- Looking ahead, what impact do you envision your product or service

having on individuals or society at large?
- How does your vision for the future align with the inspiration that initiated the development of your offering?

Personal Growth:

- How has the process of creating and developing this product or service contributed to your personal and professional growth?
- Were there moments of self-discovery or transformation during this journey?

Overcoming Challenges:

- Reflecting on challenges faced during the development phase, how did these obstacles shape the inspiration behind your offering?
- Can you share a specific instance where overcoming a challenge influenced the direction or features of your product or service?

User-Centric Approach:

- How did considerations for the end-users play a role in shaping the inspiration behind your product or service?
- Were there specific user stories or feedback that influenced the development process?

Future Aspirations:

- Looking forward, what aspirations or goals do you have for the continued evolution of your product or service?
- How does your ongoing inspiration contribute to the product roadmap and future innovations?

These questions broaden the perspective, resonating with the prospect's own challenges. The goal is to create a narrative that goes beyond a transactional relationship, connecting with the prospect's unique journey and struggles. These questions aim to unearth the rich narrative behind the producer's journey, providing a foundation for crafting compelling stories within the framework of Providence marketing.

Real-world Strategy: A tech startup soared to success by aligning its marketing strategy with the founder's vision of revolutionizing accessibility in the digital space. This alignment not only fueled their marketing efforts but also resonated with their audience.

Crafting a Compelling Narrative

The Storytelling Alchemy:

PROVIDENCE MARKETING is, at its core, storytelling. The implementation journey begins by crafting a narrative that goes beyond mere transactions. It's about weaving a tale that not only showcases the product but illuminates the journey, challenges, and victories that led to its creation. This narrative becomes the beacon that attracts like-minded individuals to join the collective journey.

Strategic Narration: An organic skincare brand elevated its market presence by narrating a story of sustainability, not just in product ingredients but in every facet of their business. This narrative captivated customers who aligned with the brand's commitment to environmental consciousness.

Highlighting Solution Impact

Illustrating Positive Transformations:

PROVIDENCE MARKETING is about showcasing the positive transformations in the producer's life. Craft narratives that illustrate how the solution became a turning point, bringing about meaningful change. These stories become beacons of hope for prospects.

Emphasizing Turning Points: Highlight the turning points and the broader impact on prospects. Whether it's improved well-being, financial stability, or personal growth, emphasize how the solution has the power to transform the lives of those who embrace it.

Showing Cost and Pain of Development

Detailed Accounts of Challenges and Costs:

TO CREATE A NARRATIVE that resonates deeply, provide detailed accounts of the challenges, costs, and emotional investment in developing the solution. Paint a vivid picture of the journey, allowing prospects to appreciate the dedication behind the product or service.

Significance in Marking a Turning Point: Emphasize the significance of revealing the cost and pain of development. This transparency not only builds credibility but also marks a turning point in the prospect's life. It becomes a sign of the providence of the producers to better the days of the prospect.

Establishing Authentic Connections

Humanizing the Brand:

IMPLEMENTATION SUCCESS hinges on humanizing the brand. Providence marketing goes beyond product-centric promotion; it's about fostering genuine connections. Authenticity becomes the currency that builds trust and credibility. Engage with your audience on a personal level, sharing not just successes but vulnerabilities, creating a relatable brand persona.

Illustrative Connection: A fitness brand strengthened its implementation strategy by showcasing not just the achievements of fitness influencers but also the struggles and setbacks they faced on their fitness journeys. This authenticity resonated with audiences seeking genuine connections.

The Providence Marketing Toolkit

Strategies for Success:

YOUR TOOLKIT FOR PROVIDENCE marketing implementation is multifaceted. It includes targeted communication, personalized narratives, and a dynamic approach to adapt to the evolving landscape. Leverage social media platforms, storytelling formats, and interactive content to amplify your message.

Toolkit in Action: A wellness company amplified its reach by utilizing a combination of blog posts, video testimonials, and engaging social media campaigns. This diversified approach ensured a comprehensive and engaging implementation strategy.

Navigating Pitfalls in Implementation

Warning Signs:

IMPLEMENTATION IS NOT without its pitfalls. Beware of overemphasis on personal success stories to the detriment of the broader narrative. Losing sight of the collective journey can erode the authenticity of your implementation efforts. Regularly assess your strategy to ensure it aligns with the producer's vision.

Real-world Caution: A financial education company faced challenges when individual success stories overshadowed the overarching mission of financial empowerment. This led to a disconnect with the audience.

Metrics for Success

Quantifying Impact:

IMPLEMENTATION SUCCESS demands a keen eye on metrics. Beyond traditional KPIs, delve into the qualitative metrics that gauge audience engagement, sentiment, and the resonance of your narrative. Track not just sales but the enduring impact on your audience's perception and loyalty. Much of these metrics has already been discussed in this book.

Key Metric: A fashion brand measured success not only by sales figures but by the number of customers actively engaging in conversations about their sustainability initiatives. This qualitative metric indicated a deeper connection with their audience.

Ongoing Optimization

Adapting to Change:

PROVIDENCE MARKETING is not static; it evolves. Regularly assess the effectiveness of your implementation strategy. Embrace feedback, adapt to industry trends, and fine-tune your approach. Optimization is a continuous journey, ensuring your narrative remains relevant and compelling.

Adaptive Strategy: An e-learning platform thrived by constantly optimizing its implementation strategy. By staying attuned to learner feedback and industry advancements, they ensured their narrative remained dynamic and engaging.

Education and Application

Helping Prospects Apply the Solution:

THE IMPLEMENTATION journey extends to helping prospects apply the solution to their current situations. Provide practical guidance and actionable steps that empower prospects to integrate the solution into their lives.

Educating Prospects to Recognize Challenges: Simultaneously, educate prospects to recognize and understand their challenges better. The marketer becomes a guide, helping prospects navigate their journey with the marketers' info package, product, service, or event.

The Emotional Resonance Factor

Beyond Transactions:

IMPLEMENTATION TRANSCENDS transactions; it's about creating emotional resonance. Monitor how your narrative resonates emotionally with your audience. An emotionally engaged audience becomes not just customers but ambassadors who willingly share your story.

Emotional Connection Example: A charitable organization implemented Providence marketing by not just showcasing their philanthropic efforts but also the transformative impact on individual lives. This emotional resonance fueled widespread support.

As we conclude this comprehensive guide to Providence marketing implementation, remember that every interaction is an opportunity to craft a narrative that resonates deeply. Your journey has just begun, and the pages ahead will explore the advanced strategies that transform Providence marketing from theory to a thriving reality.

Chapter Conclusion

This chapter has served as a compass, guiding marketers through the process of translating inspiration into action. Let's reflect on the key takeaways that illuminate the path ahead.

In crafting the producer's journey, we've discovered the power of probing questions, each one a brushstroke adding depth to the canvas of the narrative. These prompts serve as catalysts, unlocking the profound inspiration behind products and services. The tales we uncover become more than stories—they become bridges, connecting producers and prospects through shared human experiences.

Understanding the problem has evolved as a critical component of the Providence marketing story. Marketers become empathy architects by generating inquiries that delve into fundamental causes and difficulties. When this understanding is weaved into storylines, it connects deeply with prospects, building ties that go beyond basic transactions.

Highlighting the solution's impact and highlighting the expense and agony of development are critical factors that elevate the Providence marketing story. Marketers establish a route toward authenticity by showcasing good breakthroughs and discussing the hurdles overcome. The audience is transformed into participants in a journey of resilience, devotion, and eventual triumph.

This chapter's journey concludes with education and application. Marketers go from storytellers to guides, giving prospects the tools they need to apply answers to their specific problems. This educational aspect is transformative, allowing people to navigate their travels with new insights and understanding.

BOOK CONCLUSION

In Distinction marketing, the marketer tries to distinguish or separate the marketers' style and the producers' style (there is equal focus on both) in his head but delivers them as one to the prospect hence creating a situation where the prospects reasons that the seller, or marketer, and the producer are working together as one – for their benefits.

However, with Providence marketing, the primary focus is on the producer and his products and services, since it addresses the requirements and desires of the clients.

Anyone who uses the Providence marketing style and incorporates it into their marketing and sales approach will achieve significant success.

All that is required for successful Providence marketing is knowledge on the producer(s), their visions and missions, and thorough knowledge of the solution itself. Any trainings or information provided by the producer should be very well understood.

One sure benefit of the Providence marketing approach is that it makes the marketer appear like a co-owner and hence builds credibility and would help the marketer in recruitments and sub-recruitments where applicable.

GUIDE TO THE PROVIDENCE MARKETING APPROACH

1. Reveal what prompted the producer go into the production of the particular product or service. Explain what the producer believes is the cause of the particular problem in the life or body....of the prospect or adopt a wider view – in the life or body....of lots of people. After which go ahead and reveal how the solution has imparted the life of the producer(s).
2. Show the cost and pain of developing the solution and how it will mark a turning point in the life, wellbeing, and finance... of the prospect [or people] (be as specific as possible here). These will be for

signs and token of the providence of the producers to better the days of the prospect and will also go a long way to also mark a turning point in trust and participation of the prospect.

THE ABOVE TWO WOULD reveal and explain what birthed the particular solution or event and what challenges the producer faced and dealt with using the same solution plus other revelations.

On the part of the prospects, the expositions and explanations would help them come to take the solution personal – that is to apply the solution to their situation at present with a desire to go on living with the solution. The marketer would have been able to educate the prospects while helping them effectively recognize and understand their challenges better and see with the solution – the marketers' info package or product or service or event or other offering.

Below is an example to guide you in Providence marketing (this however does not replace your ability to be creative).

The producer (you may use direct names) got involved in a ghastly accident... [Give details if you know – people love stories so it is to your advantage, only respect their time and pay great attention to their body language plus be as dramatic as possible and use your senses too – once in a long while, while talking, accidentally touch the prospect for a second only if you are physically with them and it is possible to do so] **OR Here is another example:**

The producer was terribly sick... [Give details if you know] for_____ days/ weeks/months/years OR the producer [name names] was in a financial mess...[Give details if you know, and you should] for_____ days/weeks/months/ years. It is during these trying times that the producer accidentally or by chance stumbled upon_____ OR got inspiration to write_____ after_____ days/ weeks/months/years of_____. The producer thereafter started experiencing_____ with this product/service and consequently, after_____ days/weeks/months/years has decided to enrich people's lives or help who are or might be going through the same_____ [expose the problem again] to get well/ free if or when they will use_____ [The solution again]

There are more examples in the appendices that follow.

APPENDICES

APPENDICES
DEEPER DIVE INTO PROVIDENCE
MARKETING

With our Appendices section, you may go on a more in-depth examination of Providence marketing. This supplemental product is intended to help you better understand and apply this disruptive strategy. Each appendix is a wonderful resource, ranging from practical checklists to ensure full coverage to real-world case studies exemplifying success stories. Dive into a fictitious Providence marketing campaign, replete with goals and metrics, or discover handpicked readings to broaden your knowledge. Consider this area to be your toolkit, with tangible resources, examples, and suggested readings to help you along your Providence marketing journey.

APPENDIX A: Benefits and Reinforcements

As we conclude our exploration of Providence marketing, let's reinforce the profound benefits this approach can bring to your business and, more importantly, encourage you to embrace it in your strategies.

Recap of Key Concepts:

PROVIDENCE MARKETING is not just a strategy; it's a philosophy that intertwines the producer's journey with the solution's impact, creating a narrative that resonates deeply with your audience. By revealing the authentic and transformative aspects of your story, you forge a connection that transcends transactional exchanges.

Reinforcing the Benefits:

AUTHENTIC CONNECTION: Providence marketing enables you to establish authentic connections with your audience. By sharing the genuine challenges and triumphs of your journey, you build trust and credibility.

Differentiation in a Crowded Market: In a world saturated with marketing noise, Providence marketing stands out. Your unique story becomes a beacon, guiding prospects towards your brand amid the sea of options.

Building Credibility and Trust: The transparency inherent in Providence marketing positions you as not just a seller but a trusted ally. This credibility fosters long-term relationships with customers and enhances brand loyalty.

Empowering and Educating Your Audience: Providence marketing is not just about selling a product; it's about empowering and educating your audience. By showcasing the impact of your solution, you equip your customers with the knowledge to make informed decisions.

Encouraging Implementation:

NOW, THE CALL TO ACTION is clear. Take the principles of Providence marketing and integrate them into your business strategies:

Unearth Your Unique Story: Reflect on your journey as a producer. What challenges have you faced? What inspired your solution? Unearth the authentic elements of your story that can resonate with your audience.

Craft Compelling Narratives: Develop narratives that go beyond mere product descriptions. Craft stories that engage emotions and showcase the transformative power of your solution.

Share Transparently: Embrace transparency. Share both the highs and lows of your journey. Authenticity fosters a stronger connection with your audience.

Educate and Empower: Shift from a transactional mindset to an educational one. Help your audience understand not just what you sell but why it matters. Empower them to make choices aligned with their values.

In conclusion, Providence marketing isn't just a strategy; it's a transformative approach that can elevate your brand above the noise. It's an invitation to connect, resonate, and build relationships. Embrace it, weave it into your business fabric, and watch as your brand becomes not just a provider but a trusted partner in the journey of your customers. The power of Providence marketing lies in its authenticity, and the potential it holds for your business is boundless. It's time to tell your story and let it resonate with the hearts of those you aim to serve.

Appendix B: Questions to Guide You in Shaping Your Providence Marketing Strategy

YOU, AS A MARKETER, armed with a set of questions that prompts the producer to reflect on the core inspiration behind their product or service. These questions, meticulously crafted, serve as beacons that illuminate the transformative narrative, laying the foundation for a compelling marketing strategy.

Crafting effective questions requires a thoughtful approach tailored to the unique aspects of each producer's journey. However, I can provide you with a set of example questions that can serve as a starting point. These questions aim to prompt reflection on core inspirations, challenges, solutions, and emotional aspects of the producer's journey:

Core Inspirations:

a. What was the pivotal moment or inspiration that led you to create this product or service?
b. Can you share a personal story or experience that deeply influenced your decision to embark on this journey?
c. What values or beliefs drive the essence of your offerings, and how do they align with your personal mission?

Challenges and Solutions:

a. Reflecting on your journey, what were the significant challenges you faced in developing and bringing your product or service to market?
b. How did you navigate obstacles or setbacks along the way, and what lessons did you learn from those experiences?
c. Can you share a specific instance where your solution made a tangible impact on addressing a real-world problem?

Emotional Connection:

a. What moments of doubt or uncertainty did you encounter, and how did you find the resilience to move forward?

b. Describe a turning point in your journey that was emotionally significant. How did it shape your approach or perspective?

c. When reflecting on your work, what emotional highs and lows stand out the most to you?

Impact on Others:

a. Share a story or testimonial that illustrates how your product or service has positively impacted someone's life.

b. How do you envision your offerings making a lasting difference in the lives of your customers or the broader community?

c. Can you recall a moment when you received feedback that deeply resonated with you and affirmed the value of your work?

Vision for the Future:

a. Looking ahead, what is your vision for the future impact of your product or service?

b. How do you see your offerings evolving to meet the changing needs and expectations of your audience?

c. What legacy do you hope to create through your work, and how does it align with your long-term vision?

REMEMBER, THE EFFECTIVENESS of these questions lies in their ability to evoke genuine and thoughtful responses. Feel free to adapt and customize them according to the particular circumstances and peculiarities of the producer's story.

Appendix C: Strategies for Acquiring Comprehensive Knowledge of the Solution

IN THE REALM OF PROVIDENCE marketing, where understanding the solution is paramount, employing effective strategies to acquire comprehensive knowledge is the linchpin of success. As an experienced marketer and salesman, consider these strategies to go deeply into the details of the solution to guarantee a thoughtful and detailed integration strategy:

1. Immerse Yourself in the Product/Service:

    a. Spend time actively using, experiencing, or testing the product or service.

    b. Engage in hands-on exploration to grasp its functionality, features, and unique attributes.

    c. Immerse yourself in the user experience to understand both its strengths and potential pain points.

2. Collaborate with Producers and Experts:

    a. Foster open communication channels with producers and subject matter experts.

    b. Arrange regular meetings or workshops to discuss the solution in detail.

    c. Encourage producers to share insights, technical details, and the underlying philosophy of the solution.

3. Leverage Training and Educational Resources:

    a. Utilize any training programs, workshops, or educational materials provided by the producer.

    b. Attend webinars, conferences, or industry events related to the product/service.

    c. Ensure team members have access to comprehensive training resources to enhance their understanding.

4. Conduct In-Depth Research:

a. Dive into research materials, industry publications, and case studies related to the solution.
b. Explore academic papers, whitepapers, and authoritative sources to gain a theoretical understanding.
c. Keep abreast of the latest trends, advancements, and innovations in the field.

5. Seek Customer Feedback and Testimonials:

a. Connect with existing customers to gather their feedback and testimonials.
b. Understand how the solution has impacted their lives or businesses.
c. Analyze customer reviews and testimonials to identify patterns and common themes.

6. Collaborate with Customer Support and Sales Teams:

a. Work closely with customer support teams to understand common queries and challenges.
b. Collaborate with the sales team to gain insights into customer needs and objections.
c. Leverage frontline interactions to gather real-world anecdotes and experiences.

7. Conduct Surveys and Feedback Sessions:

a. Design surveys to collect feedback from users and potential customers.
b. Organize feedback sessions or focus groups to gather qualitative insights.
c. Use the data collected to identify areas of improvement and better understand customer perceptions.

8. Analyze Competitor Offerings:

   a. Study competitor products or services within the same niche.
   b. Identify unique selling points, competitive advantages, and areas for differentiation.
   c. Analyzing the competitive landscape provides a broader context for understanding the solution.

9. Stay Updated on Industry Trends:

   a. Subscribe to industry publications, blogs, and newsletters to stay informed.
   b. Follow thought leaders, influencers, and key players in the industry on social media.
   c. Embrace a continuous learning mindset to adapt to evolving industry trends.

10. Develop Cross-Functional Teams:

   a. Form cross-functional teams comprising members from different departments.
   b. Encourage collaboration between marketing, sales, product development, and customer support.
   c. Foster a holistic understanding of the solution by leveraging diverse perspectives.

BY EMPLOYING THESE comprehensive strategies, you position yourself to gain a profound understanding of the solution, laying the groundwork for successful Providence marketing integration.

Appendix D: Providence Marketing Checklist

Use this checklist to ensure you've covered key aspects when implementing Providence marketing in your strategy:

Producer's Journey:

a. Unearth the challenges faced by the producer.
b. Identify the turning points that led to the creation of your solution.

Crafting Compelling Narratives:

a. Develop narratives that engage emotions.
b. Ensure your stories highlight the transformative impact of your solution.

Transparency and Authenticity:

a. Share both successes and challenges transparently.
b. Build authenticity into your communication strategy.

Educational Approach:

a. Shift from a transactional mindset to an educational one.
b. Provide resources that empower your audience to make informed decisions.

Empathy and Connection:

a. Show empathy towards the challenges your audience faces.
b. Establish a genuine connection by aligning your values with those of your audience.

Integration with Business Goals:

a. Ensure that your Providence marketing efforts align with broader business objectives.
b. Measure the impact of your strategy on key performance indicators.

Appendix E: Providence Marketing Samples and Case Studies

LET'S EXPLORE SITUATIONS where Providence marketing comes to life:

Example 1: The Healing Journey of Wellness Guru Sarah Johnson

SARAH JOHNSON, A WELL-known wellness guru, faced a health crisis that shook the foundations of her vibrant life. For over six months, Sarah battled a mysterious ailment that left her physically drained and emotionally exhausted. It was during these trying times that she serendipitously stumbled upon ancient holistic practices during her travels.

Inspired by her newfound wellness regimen, Sarah not only regained her health but discovered a profound calling to share this transformative journey. After years of applying these practices, she decided to enrich the lives of others facing health challenges. Her product, a comprehensive wellness guide and a line of natural supplements, became a beacon of hope for those seeking a holistic approach to well-being.

Example 2: Financial Maestro James Thornton's Triumph Over Adversity

JAMES THORNTON, A FINANCIAL expert, found himself in the midst of a financial downturn that spanned several months. A series of unfortunate events left his once-thriving business on the brink of collapse. During this financial crisis, James stumbled upon innovative investment strategies that not only lifted him out of the financial mess but opened new avenues for prosperity.

Motivated by his journey from financial struggle to success, James decided to share his insights. He wrote a comprehensive guide detailing his financial strategies and launched a series of workshops to help others navigate similar challenges. The Providence marketing in his approach lies in revealing the trials he faced, showcasing the tangible benefits of his solution, and offering a pathway for others to achieve financial freedom.

Example 3: The Inspirational Tale of Tech Innovator Mark Turner

MARK TURNER, A TECH innovator, found himself grappling with a prolonged creative block that hindered his ability to develop groundbreaking solutions. For months, Mark faced the challenge of navigating through a creative drought, unable to harness the innovative spirit that once defined his work. During a period of introspection and self-discovery, Mark stumbled upon an unconventional source of inspiration – nature.

Drawn to the intricate patterns and efficiency of natural systems, Mark experienced a reawakening of his creativity. This newfound perspective not only revitalized his work but sparked the creation of revolutionary tech solutions inspired by the brilliance of the natural world. Mark, transformed by this experience, decided to share his journey with the world. His Providence marketing approach involves unveiling the struggle, showcasing the catalyst for inspiration, and offering tech solutions that echo the efficiency of nature.

Example 4: Financial Consultant Olivia Rodriguez's Empowerment Odyssey

OLIVIA RODRIGUEZ, A financial consultant, faced a personal journey of empowerment after enduring a challenging period of self-doubt and financial instability. For an extended period, Olivia grappled with feelings of inadequacy and the weight of financial burdens. It was during this emotionally charged time that Olivia stumbled upon empowering mindset techniques and financial strategies that turned her life around.

Motivated by her transformation, Olivia dedicated herself to empowering others facing similar struggles. She wrote a book detailing her journey, offering practical financial advice, and conducting workshops to foster financial literacy and empowerment. Olivia's Providence marketing strategy involves laying bare her vulnerabilities, showcasing the impact of her solution, and empowering others to take control of their financial destinies.

These examples emphasize the versatility of Providence marketing, demonstrating how personal challenges can become powerful narratives of inspiration, leading to the development of transformative solutions that enrich the lives of others.

Appendix F: Providence Marketing Flow

IN THIS REPRESENTATION, each step in the Providence marketing process is outlined. From the initial challenge faced by the producer to the revelation of their journey, crafting narratives, and ultimately empowering others, the flow captures the essence of how Providence marketing unfolds. Please note that this is a simplified representation, and another implementation may involve more detailed interactions and strategies.

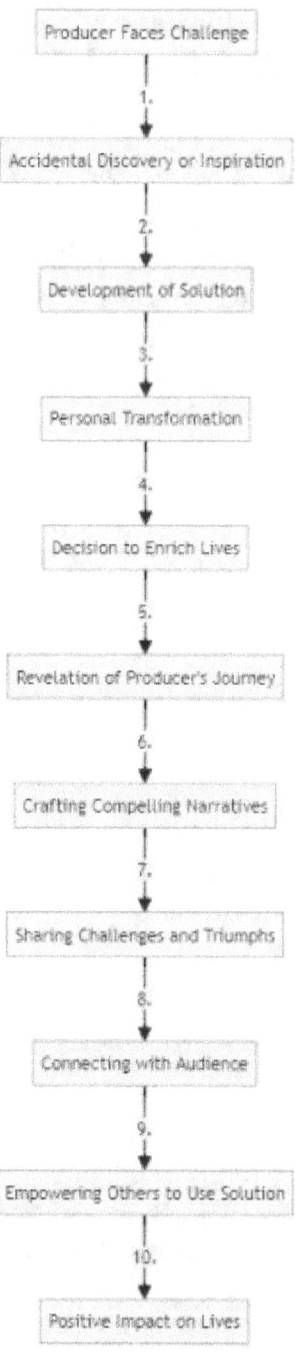

Appendix G: Case Studies

THE CASE STUDIES SECTION of this toolkit delves into real-world examples that illustrate the successful application of Providence marketing in various contexts. These case studies provide valuable insights, practical lessons, and tangible outcomes achieved by organizations that embraced the full principles of Providence marketing.

1. Tom's Shoes: Walking for a Cause

CONTEXT: Tom's Shoes has redefined the traditional business model by incorporating a one-for-one giving approach. For every pair of shoes sold, another is donated to a child in need. This Providence marketing strategy not only addresses a pressing social issue but also engages consumers emotionally, making them active participants in a mission to improve lives. The success lies not just in sales but in creating a community that feels a genuine connection with the brand's humanitarian mission.

2. Dove's Real Beauty Campaign: Redefining Beauty Standards

CONTEXT: Dove's Real Beauty campaign exemplifies Providence marketing by addressing societal norms and empowering individuals. By focusing on promoting diverse representations of beauty, Dove aimed to inspire confidence and self-esteem. The campaign resonated globally, sparking conversations and making Dove not just a soap brand but a champion for authenticity and self-acceptance.

3. Patagonia: Wearing Responsibility

CONTEXT: Patagonia, the outdoor clothing company, stands out for its commitment to environmental responsibility. Through its "Worn Wear" initiative, Patagonia encourages customers to buy used Patagonia gear or trade in their old items. This approach aligns with Providence marketing principles by emphasizing sustainability, responsible consumption, and the longevity of products, fostering a community dedicated to environmental stewardship.

4. Warby Parker: Clear Vision, Clear Purpose

CONTEXT: Warby Parker disrupted the eyewear industry by blending commerce with a social mission. For every pair of glasses sold, Warby Parker donates a pair to someone in need. This Providence marketing strategy not only addresses the lack of access to eyewear but also positions Warby Parker as a brand with a clear purpose. This approach not only attracts customers but also builds trust and loyalty by making them part of a meaningful cause.

5. TOMRA: The Reverse Vending Revolution

CONTEXT: TOMRA, a global leader in reverse vending solutions, turns the act of recycling into a rewarding experience. By implementing machines that collect used beverage containers and provide a refund, TOMRA aligns with Providence marketing principles. The initiative not only contributes to environmental sustainability but also engages consumers actively in the recycling process, fostering a sense of shared responsibility.

These real-world examples showcase how organizations across diverse industries have embraced Providence marketing to create meaningful connections, address social or environmental challenges, and redefine their roles beyond mere transactions. The outcomes go beyond financial success, manifesting in stronger brand loyalty, community engagement, and a positive impact on society.

Appendix H: Further Reading

IF YOU'RE KEEN ON DELVING deeper into Providence marketing and related concepts, here are some recommended readings:

a. **"Start with Why: How Great Leaders Inspire Everyone to Take Action" by Simon Sinek**

Explore the foundational principles of understanding and communicating the purpose behind your endeavors.

a. **"Building a StoryBrand: Clarify Your Message So Customers Will Listen" by Donald Miller**

Gain insights into creating a compelling narrative that resonates with your audience and fosters engagement.

a. "The Thank You Economy" by Gary Vaynerchuk

Discover the importance of building authentic relationships in the digital age and how gratitude can be a powerful marketing tool.

a. "Conscious Capitalism: Liberating the Heroic Spirit of Business" by John Mackey and Raj Sisodia

Explore the idea of businesses operating with a higher purpose and how it can lead to long-term success.

a. "Firms of Endearment: How World-Class Companies Profit from Passion and Purpose" by Raj Sisodia, Jagdish N. Sheth, and David B. Wolfe

Delve into case studies of companies that have successfully integrated purpose and profitability.

a. "To Sell is Human: The Surprising Truth About Moving Others" by Daniel H. Pink

Gain insights into the art and science of selling in a world where everyone is essentially in the business of moving others.

a. "Blue Ocean Strategy: How to Create Uncontested Market Space and Make Competition Irrelevant" by W. Chan Kim and Renée Mauborgne

Explore strategies for innovation and creating new market spaces that align with Providence marketing's focus on differentiation.

Appendix I: Glossary of Terms

HERE'S A GLOSSARY OF terms related to Providence marketing and associated concepts:

Providence Marketing: A strategic approach where the producer and their products or services take center stage, emphasizing a purpose-driven narrative and building meaningful connections with customers.

Distinction Marketing: A marketing strategy that aims to separate the styles of the marketer and the producer in the marketer's mind, often focusing on the marketer's unique selling points.

Producer-Centric Approach: A philosophy that places the producer and their vision at the forefront, recognizing the significance of their journey and mission in shaping the marketing strategy.

Core Principles: Fundamental beliefs and values that guide the implementation of Providence marketing, often involving authenticity, purpose, and customer-centricity.

Integrated Storytelling: The practice of weaving a cohesive and compelling narrative that aligns with the producer's journey and resonates with the audience, fostering a deeper connection.

One-for-One Giving: A philanthropic model where a company donates a product or service for each one sold, contributing to a social or environmental cause.

Sustainability: A commitment to practices that ensure the long-term well-being of the environment, society, and business, often associated with responsible sourcing and production.

Community Engagement: Involving and interacting with the audience on a deeper level, fostering a sense of community and shared values.

Brand Loyalty: The degree of commitment and attachment a customer feels towards a brand, often influenced by positive experiences and shared values.

Conscious Capitalism: A business philosophy emphasizing the importance of aligning profit-making activities with ethical and socially responsible practices.

Customer-Centricity: A business approach where the customer's needs, preferences, and experience are prioritized in product development, marketing, and overall strategy.

In-Depth Knowledge: Comprehensive understanding of the producer(s), their visions, missions, and the solutions they offer, forming the foundation of effective Providence marketing.

Empathy: The ability to understand and share the feelings of another, crucial in connecting with customers on a personal level.

Data-Driven Insights: Utilizing data and analytics to make informed decisions and optimize marketing strategies for better results.

Alliance Building: The art of forming partnerships and collaborations that complement each partner's strengths, contributing to mutual success.

Brand Perception: How a brand is perceived by customers, influenced by the brand's values, actions, and the overall customer experience.

Recruitment and Sub-Recruitment: The process of attracting and engaging individuals to join the brand's mission, expanding its reach through a network of advocates.

Implementation: The practical application of Providence marketing strategies in day-to-day business operations.

Metrics and KPIs: Quantifiable measures used to assess the effectiveness of Providence marketing, including customer engagement, brand loyalty, and revenue growth.

Thank You Economy: A business approach emphasizing gratitude and genuine appreciation as a key component of customer interactions and relationship-building.

This glossary aims to provide clarity on terms related to Providence marketing and its associated principles, strategies, and philosophies.

Appendix J: Author's Notes and Insights

DEAR READER,

Embarking on the journey of Providence marketing has been a profound exploration into the heart of business, purpose, and connection. In these notes, I offer insights to complement the pages you've just turned, providing a glimpse into the inspiration and intention behind this exploration.

Unveiling Purpose:

Providence marketing is more than a strategy; it's a philosophy that invites businesses to unearth their purpose. As you dive into these pages, consider the profound impact of aligning your mission with your customers' needs. Purpose isn't a luxury but a necessity for sustained success.

The Power of Stories:

Throughout this book, you'll notice a recurring theme—stories. Stories are bridges that connect us, and in Providence marketing, they are catalysts for meaningful connections. Behind every product or service lies a narrative waiting to be told, one that resonates with the human experience.

Empathy as Currency:

Amidst the strategies and principles, never underestimate the currency of empathy. Understanding the struggles, joys, and aspirations of your audience is a cornerstone of Providence marketing. Empathy builds trust, and trust is the bedrock of enduring relationships.

From Transaction to Transformation:

As you absorb the content, challenge yourself to move beyond the transactional mindset. Providence marketing propels businesses into the realm of transformation, where every interaction contributes to a profound change, not just for the customer but for the business itself.

An Ongoing Conversation:

Consider this book as a conversation starter. The ideas presented are not final statements but invitations for you to reflect, adapt, and apply in the context of your unique journey. Providence marketing is a living concept, evolving with every business that embraces it.

Implementing Providence marketing:

The Guide to Providence marketing Implementation is your practical toolkit. Each section is a compass guiding you through the intricate landscape of purpose-driven marketing. Remember, implementation is where philosophy transforms into action.

A Call to Action:

In the spirit of Providence marketing, I encourage you to take action. Whether you're a seasoned entrepreneur or a budding innovator, infuse purpose into every facet of your business. The impact goes beyond profit; it's about leaving a meaningful mark on the world.

Thank you for joining me on this odyssey. May the principles of Providence marketing illuminate your path toward a business that transcends mere transactions and becomes a force for positive change.

Warm regards,

Eugy Enoch.

Appendix K: Contacts and Connect

AT THE HEART OF ANY knowledge exchange is the opportunity to connect. In this final appendix, you'll find contact information, social media profiles, and platforms where you can engage with me, the author, and with fellow readers who share your passion for reveal marketing. It's a space to foster connections, share ideas, and continue the dialogue beyond the pages of this book.

I invite you to reach out and connect with me if you have any questions, insights, or thoughts to share about the world of Reveal Marketing. I am excited to continue this conversation beyond the pages of this book and explore how we can further enhance our understanding and application of these strategies.

Author Contact

You can find me on various social media platforms, where I regularly share insights, updates, and engage in meaningful discussions. Feel free to connect and follow to stay updated on the latest trends and developments in the field of marketing:

X(formerly, Twitter): @eugyenoch[1]
Instagram: @eugyenoch[2]
LinkedIn: https://www.linkedin.com/in/eugyenoch
Facebook: https://www.facebook.com/eugyenoch
Wattpad: https://www.wattpad.com/user/eugyenoch
Substack: https://substack.com/@eugyenoch
Goodreads: https://goodreads.com/eugyenoch

I am genuinely excited to connect with fellow marketers, professionals, and enthusiasts who are passionate about the art of crafting compelling narratives and creating authentic connections with audiences. Your insights and experiences are valuable, and I look forward to engaging with you in this exciting journey.

---

1.   https://www.x.com/eugyenoch

2.   https://www.instagram.com/eugyenoch

Feel free to drop me a message, share your thoughts, or ask questions. Let's continue to learn, grow, and evolve together in the ever-changing landscape of marketing.

Best regards,

Eugy Enoch.

In Closing

In closing, as we conclude this exploration into Providence marketing, I extend my heartfelt gratitude for joining me on this journey. We've delved into the heart of purpose-driven business, uncovering the transformative potential that lies within each interaction, each story, and each connection.

Providence marketing is more than a strategy; it's a call to infuse meaning into every facet of your business. As you step forward, armed with the insights, strategies, and real-world examples shared in these pages, I encourage you to be a beacon of purpose in the business landscape.

Remember, the journey doesn't end here. It continues with every decision, every campaign, and every interaction. May your business be a testament to the power of aligning mission with impact, and may you find fulfillment in the positive change you bring to the world.

Thank you for entrusting me with your time and attention. May your path be illuminated with purpose, and may your endeavors be a force for good in the tapestry of business.

YOUR NOTES

About the Author

'Eugy' Enoch, is an experienced, talented, and remarkable leader who is dedicated to maintaining cutting-edge technical and interpersonal skills as well as industry expertise. He possesses exceptional relationship-building, training, and presenting skills, as well as the ability to juggle several responsibilities. Broad industry experience includes Digital marketing, Software development, Education, Books, Media, Administration, and Charity.

About the Publisher

Iboora Library Publications, is your literary ally, dedicated to turning stories into reality. Our team of experts ensures your work meets the highest quality standards and reaches a broad audience. Whether you're an aspiring author or an established one, we offer flexible publishing options to suit your vision. We're more than a publisher; we're your literary partner, bringing your stories to life and advocating for your creativity. Join us on this storytelling adventure, where every page holds a new world, and every book is a testament to your talent.

Read more at https://iboora.com.

www.ingramcontent.com/pod-product-compliance
Lightning Source LLC
Chambersburg PA
CBHW062332290526
45794CB00005B/1999